Petro-Pirates

Peter Corris is a writer best known for his books about Sydney private eye, Cliff Hardy. He collaborated with the late Fred Hollows, environmentalist John Sinclair and actor Ray Barrett in the writing of their autobiographies. Married to the writer Jean Bedford, he is an Adjunct professor in the School of Humanities, Media and Cultural Studies at Southern Cross University, Lismore and lives at Byron Bay on the far north coast of New South Wales.

Petro-Pirates

The hijacking of the Petro Ranger

Captain Ken Blyth

with Peter Corris

ALLEN & UNWIN

First published in 2000 by
Allen & Unwin
9 Atchison Street
St Leonards NSW 2065
Australia
Phone: (61 2) 8425 0100
Fax: (61 2) 9906 2218
E-mail: frontdesk@allen-unwin.com.au
Web: http://www.allen-unwin.com.au

National Library of Australia
Cataloguing-in-Publication entry:

Blyth, Ken.
  Petro-pirates: the hijacking of the Petro Ranger.

  Includes index.
  ISBN 1 86508 368 2.

  1. Blyth, Ken. 2. MT Petro Ranger (Ships). 3. Pirates—
Singapore Strait. 4. Ship captains—Australia. I. Corris,
Peter, 1942– . II. Title.

910.450916472

Set in 11/13pt Arrus by DOCUPRO, Sydney
Printed and bound by Griffin Press Pty Ltd, South Australia

10 9 8 7 6 5 4 3 2 1

Dedicated to all seafarers killed by pirates, and their grieving families.

For help in the preparation of this book, thanks to my wife and daughters.

Contents

PETRO-PIRATES

Illustrations

Prologue

A slow start in Singapore

After 38 years as a merchant seaman working in different parts of the world, I must have seen thousands of cargoes loaded and unloaded. Mostly the work goes smoothly, occasionally there are mishaps. During loading the members of the crew have their various duties but the master of the vessel has the ultimate responsibility. His command starts here—before the voyage actually begins.

On being appointed to a ship, the Captain automatically accepts overall responsibility for both the crew and the operations they carry out as well as for the ship itself. He is also solely accountable to the owners of the ship for all business carried out on their behalf whilst in port. Not only does the Captain have to have a sound knowledge of ship operations, he also has to have a good working knowledge of the law dealing with his area of shipping, as a signature in the wrong place or on the wrong document can cost the shipowner vast sums of money. In simple terms, I suppose you could liken him to a floating CEO of a small company coupled with being the Mayor of a small town.

To assist him in running the ship, which is divided into three departments, he has the Chief Officer who is head of the deck/radio department, and second-in-command of the ship. The Chief Engineer is the head of the engineering department, including electrical systems. The Cook looks after the catering department, but keeps the Captain advised constantly of the principal activities relating to his job, as he is not classed as an Officer. All departments are staffed by Officers and ratings and a brief outline of their duties follows:

Chief Officer: Head of the deck department—responsible for stability, cargo, cargo operations, deck maintenance programmes and the work carried out by the ratings working under the Bosun (deck foreman). Importantly, he is responsible for ensuring the ship has sufficient fresh water on board for the voyage prior to departure, checking daily on amounts used and the remaining on board (ROB) figure. He is the officer of the watch (4–8) when the ship is at sea and in port is responsible for all cargo operations and safety requirements needed for this activity.

Second Officer: He is the navigating officer and is responsible for voyage planning, i.e., charts, courses, calculating distances. He is the officer in charge of the 12–4 watch. In port he is responsible to the Chief Officer and is in charge of cargo operations for 12 hours per day. He is also the medical officer, under the Captain's supervision.

Third Officer: He is the junior officer and in charge of the 8–12 watch at sea. His prime responsibility is safety-officer, and to ensure that everything from lifeboats to fire-fighting equipment is in good working order at all times.

Radio Officer: Responsible for radio equipment but at the end of 1998 became redundant, all radio work being incorporated with the deck-officer's duties. No radio messages can be sent without the Captain's authorisation.

At sea, one of the above officers is on watch on the bridge at all times, with a seaman joining them at night carrying out the duty of additional look-out.

The balance of the deck ratings work on deck maintenance under the supervision of the Bosun (deck foreman) and generally work from 7 a.m. to 5 p.m. with one hour off for each meal. In port, deck ratings are split in number and keep 12-hour cargo watches, also taking stores, fuel and fresh water on board.

Engineering Department

Chief Engineer: Has full responsibility to the Captain for this department and his job, to a great extent, is an administrative one. He is the senior technical person on the ship.

At sea, in the engine room (if not automated) the second Engineer keeps the 4–8 watch, the Third Engineer the 12–4 watch and the Fourth Engineer the 8–12 watch. An engine room rating is on duty with the engineer at all times during these watches.

The balance of the engine room ratings work the same day hours as the deck ratings, but in the engine room. In port, the full staff are employed on main engine maintenance while it is stopped and a Duty Engineer is on call 24 hours a day.

The Cook has probably one of the most important jobs on the ship. If you are unlucky and get a bad cook, the ship tends to be an unhappy one and a bad cook is usually the first one to be sacked, as with a good cook you have a contented crew and a happy one.

As Captain, my main function in port is dealing with the various Port Authorities, of which there are many, duties. No radio messages can be sent without the Captain's authorisation.

At sea, one of the above officers is on watch on the bridge at all times, with a seaman joining them at night carrying out the duty of additional look-out.

The balance of the deck ratings work on deck maintenance under the supervision of the Bosun (deck foreman) and generally work from 7 a.m. to 5 p.m. with one hour off for each meal. In port, deck ratings are split in number and keep 12-hour cargo watches, also taking stores, fuel and fresh water on board.

Engineering Department

Chief Engineer: Has full responsibility to the Captain for this department and his job, to a great extent, is an administrative one. He is the senior technical person on the ship.

At sea, in the engine room (if not automated) the second Engineer keeps the 4–8 watch, the Third Engineer the 12–4 watch and the Fourth Engineer the 8–12 watch. An engine room rating is on duty with the engineer at all times during these watches.

The balance of the engine room ratings work the same day hours as the deck ratings, but in the engine room. In port, the full staff are employed on main engine maintenance while it is stopped and a Duty Engineer is on call 24 hours a day.

The Cook has probably one of the most important jobs on the ship. If you are unlucky and get a bad cook, the ship tends to be an unhappy one and a bad cook is usually the first one to be sacked, as with a good cook you have a contented crew and a happy one.

As Captain, my main function in port is dealing with the various Port Authorities, of which there are many, keeping the Company's Head Office advised of up-to-date events and, prior to departure, double-checking the stability, fuel and fresh water totals as well as going over the navigation plans. Final weather reports are always checked. Even on departure or arrival in port, with a Harbour Pilot onboard, the Captain still has overall command.

At sea, it's as any Manager's role, i.e., continually checking all departments are working efficiently, dealing with complaints and, of course, with total responsibility for discipline. Then we have the dreaded paperwork, as in recent times Procedure Manuals have been generated and have to be administered.

I am on call 24 hours per day in case of an emergency and on approaching or leaving a port I am always on the bridge. Also at sea, if restricted visibility sets in, I am on the bridge until the weather clears.

Once a day I would have a meeting with the Chief Officer and Chief Engineer to discuss the day's work and assist where possible if any unforeseen problems arose. But, if the ship is well run and the men happy, it makes a Captain's job a lot easier and one is continuously on the lookout for any friction developing between any crew members. This must be nipped in the bud quickly, as with people being together and isolated for many days, small things can develop into big things very quickly. Generally, this occurs very occasionally.

On 15 April 1998 I was the Captain of MT *Petro Ranger*, which was berthed at the Shell Petroleum Company's Bukum terminal in Singapore. The *Petro Ranger* (the MT stands for 'Motor Tanker' as distinct from the standard MV, 'Motor Vessel', and indicates that the ship carries a flammable cargo), was a modern tanker built in 1993 and equipped with the latest technology for loading, storage, navigation and communication. At a length of 128 metres she was small as tankers go, but she was a fine vessel.

Owned by Petroships, a Singaporean company, but registered in Malaysia for commercial reasons, she was one of a fleet of small- to medium-sized tankers transporting fuel around an area that was experiencing economic turmoil. The 'tiger economies' of South-East Asia had ceased to roar.

For that voyage our cargo was 9600 tonnes of automotive diesel oil and 1600 tonnes of jet fuel. First time up, the loading of a tanker is an alarming event. I remember thinking, *My God, this only needs a spark* when I first experienced the fumes and gases and was aware of them seeping into the airconditioning and other systems. But, in fact, with all safety measures properly observed, a sea tanker isn't a dangerous craft. It's safer than a road tanker barrelling down a highway, and I had many years under my belt delivering these volatile cargoes safely to their destinations.

Having dealt with practically every major petroleum company in operation, I'd found Shell to be perhaps the most efficient, so I was surprised at Bukum to encounter delays and difficulties. The loading took twelve hours longer than it should have. With our modern equipment the problem could not be at our end, and my increasingly testy enquiries met with less than satisfactory answers. *Captain, the shore tanks have low levels. Sorry. Captain, apologies, the shore pumps are also being used to transfer fuel within the refinery.*

In my experience, to fret about what you cannot control is a waste of energy. Patience is a virtue at sea and a requirement in South-East Asia where the pace of things may not always suit the European temperament. Safety and efficiency count for more than precise schedules in the ticklish business of transporting fuel, so I saved my breath and attended to my duties.[1]

Eventually, at 3.00 p.m. on 16 April, the loading was completed and 30 minutes later the documentation was brought on board for my signature. I signed bills of lading which testified to the ownership of the

PETRO-PIRATES

SHIP'S PARTICULARS

M.T. PETRO RANGER

FLAG	: MALAYSIA	PORT OF REGISTRY	: PORT KELANG
OFFICIAL NO.	: 327292	CALL SIGN	: 9MCI5
IMO NO.	: 7115086		

Deadweight	Tropical : 12,751 tonnes Summer : 12,357 tonnes	Main Engine	: 'Kobe Hatsudoki (Mitsubishi) 6UEC 52/105D 1 x 6200 PS
Draft/Displacement	: Tropical : 8.17 m/16,118 tonnes Summer : 7.99 m/15,724 tonnes Light : 1.929m/ 3,367 tonnes	Boiler	: 1 x Osaka Composite boiler
Built	: January 1993		
Builders	: Pan-United Shipyard Singapore	Cargo Pumps	: Taiko Screw 2 x 750 m³/hr
Class	: N.K. (Ocean-going)	Cargo Piping System	: Ring Main with double valve segregation
Next Special Survey	: January 1998	Speed	: 13 knots
Gross Tons	: 6,718	Bunker Capacity	: 80 m³ (MDO) 800m³ (FO)
Net Tons	: 4,023		

Dimension -
  Length
  Breadth
  Depth
	: 128.00 metres (o.a.)
	: 21.0 metres
	: 10.04 metres
		Fresh Water Capacity	: 220 m³

		Navigational Aids	: Radar, gyro compass, direction finder, echo sounder, GPS, speedlog, sat. nav.
Cargo Tanks	: 6 tanks (12 compartments)		
Cubic Capacity	: 14,005 m³	Radio Equipment	: GMDSS for A3 area Immarsat M&C

	Port (m³)	Stbd (m³)			
Tank No. 1	: 790	791	LSA	:	35 persons
Tank No. 2	1,081	1,083			
Tank No. 3	1,363	1,366			
Tank No. 4	1,362	1,364			
Tank No. 5	1,090	1,092			
Tank No. 6	1,311	1,312			
Total	6,997	7,008			

Tank Coating	: Epoxy	

Particulars believed to be correct but not guaranteed

1. The ship's particulars for the MT *Petro Ranger*.

cargo, valued at $A2.3 million, certification of export permits and documents detailing the quantity and nature of the cargo. The paperwork unavoidably goes with the territory, and is a far cry from the old days of chalk marks on the sides of crates and handshakes over a glass of rum.

At 4.15 p.m., Shell's harbour pilot boarded and we undocked. We were flying the distinctive Malaysian flag—yellow sun and crescent on a blue background with red and white stripes—as we made the ten-minute run out to the Sisters Buoy in Singapore Harbour.

The pilot seemed very annoyed at the delay. 'Have a safe voyage, Captain.'

Why not? I thought as I farewelled the pilot. His tone had been sarcastic and I wondered about it later.

PART I

An act of piracy

1

On course for Saigon*

Indeed there was every reason to anticipate a good voyage. I'd made the same trip—the destination was Saigon in Vietnam—only a few weeks before without incident. This would be the last run of my current stint. I was booked to fly home to Australia on 23 April for a spell of leave during which I'd celebrate my 53rd birthday and, more importantly, my silver wedding anniversary.

They were pleasant prospects but meantime there was the considerable responsibility of getting the ship clear of the harbour. Singapore Harbour and the Singapore Straits are one of the busiest waterways on earth with craft varying from giant supertankers of 250 000 tonnes to small coastal craft. The large vessels keep to the assigned lanes (known as traffic separation lanes) and their movements can be anticipated, but the smaller ones obey no known rules and expect other ships to avoid them. Consequently, when negotiating

---

* On my first visit to Vietnam, the authorities there explained to me that 'Saigon' was the working name of the city and 'Ho Chi Minh City' was the political name. On official documentation 'Ho Chi Minh City' was used but the residents of the city and most of the population of the nation still called the city 'Saigon'. I could clearly see that boats in the harbour were registered under and carrying that name.

the Straits, I kept the *Petro Ranger* on light fuel to maintain her manoeuvrability.

The weather was in our favour; it was a balmy tropical afternoon shading into evening, as we crossed the Singapore Straits in the eastbound traffic lane making for the Horseboro Light, which signified the open sea. As I said, the *Petro Ranger* was a comfortable ship, airconditioned with coffee-making facilities on the bridge, finely responsive equipment and superb visibility. Nevertheless, spending five hours on the bridge (with only a ten-minute break in my cabin during a quiet period to eat some sandwiches) with the ship under manual control amounts to hard work and I wasn't sorry to reach the Horseboro Light at 9.30 p.m. and be able to set a course for our destination.

Working in the South China Sea is not like cruising Sydney Harbour. The area is subject to violent typhoons, although not in April. The chief danger is human. Like the Spanish Main in days gone by, the South China Sea has become notorious for pirates. The International Chamber of Commerce (ICC) International Maritime Bureau compiles data on piracy and its report for 1998 detailed seven attacks between January and the date of my voyage in the waters in which I was sailing.[2] The most serious was the assault on the Honduran tanker *Tioman* off Malaysia on 11 January. Armed with rifles and knives, pirates boarded the vessel, beat up the crew and locked them in a cabin. All communications equipment that couldn't be removed was destroyed, cash and personal effects were stolen and a million litres of fuel was transferred to another tanker before the pirates departed. Although at that time I wasn't aware of this particular event, I was mindful of the danger and when I wrote out my night orders, which each officer was required to read and sign on taking over his watch, I stressed that an alert pirate watch was to be maintained. I also made the point verbally to the officer of

4

the watch and requested him to do the same when he was relieved.

The *Petro Ranger* carried no firearms in the sensible belief that for merchant ships to go armed would only cause violently disposed pirates to up the ante. The danger of using firearms aboard a tanker, not to mention grenades, which would be a logical consequence of such an escalation, hardly needs stressing. Precaution and deterrent were the watchwords. It was standard practice for all doors to accommodation spaces on the ship to be locked internally so that access to the interior could only be obtained through the bridge doors, which had to remain open for lookout duties and navigational purposes. In the event of suspicious craft approaching, the drill was for a vessel to alter course, continually sound its whistle and alarm bells and send out a signal for assistance required due to suspected pirate attack on the VHF radio. In those busy waters this was thought to be sufficient protection against attack providing that those on watch were alert, quick, cool-headed and resourceful.

After satisfying myself that all was well and that there was no close shipping to be concerned about, I bade the Third Officer goodnight and went down to my cabin. It had been a long day with a certain amount of frustration involved but, with the ship handling well and good weather forecast, I had no reason to anticipate anything but a successful conclusion to the day. Or so I thought.

The Captain's quarters consisted of a suite: a bedroom with a double bed (the only one on the ship), wardrobe and chest of drawers and a bathroom; and a day room fitted up as an office-cum-sitting room with a desk and chair, easy chairs and settee, and a television set and VCR. Also there was a bar fridge, although it's worth noting that the *Petro Ranger*, in accordance with the Islamic law of the country of its registration, carried no alcohol. Although I am a social drinker, this prohibition was no inconvenience to me. Throughout my maritime career I've made it a practice to 'take the pledge' at the beginning of every voyage.

On joining Petroships on 30 December 1997, I was fortunate in that the vessel I was to command, the MT *Petro Ranger*, was in dry-dock in Singapore for 10 days. This gave me the opportunity to visit the company's head office frequently to pick up on all the small operational and accounting procedures that vary from company to company. Also, it gave the office staff and myself the chance to familiarise ourselves on a personal basis, rather than just being voices on the telephone and names on faxes. Usually, a new captain spends one day in the company's office prior to joining his ship and then he's off on his own.

Employment practices in shipping have changed radically over the past fifteen years. In my opinion, in South-East Asia, the trend now is for crew to be regarded as an unfortunate, but unavoidable expense. Australia works under an Award system in which generally favourable conditions of service are laid down. But, in South-East Asia, captains, officers and crew are employed under contract. I was able to negotiate a contract acceptable to myself; other ranks generally were obliged to accept whatever was offered under contracts of varying lengths.

Petroships had a high level of re-engagement for several reasons. One was that the company's ships operated in the area the crews were drawn from and home leave and communications were possible. Secondly, given the economic crisis that hit the area, particularly Indonesia and Malaysia in the late 1990s, the Singapore dollar remained relatively strong. Petroships paid salaries directly into bank accounts in that currency and its employees benefited from the favourable exchange rate.

Bangladesh has always been drawn on by Malaysia and Singapore as a source of cheap 'guest' labour and ships' crews. A high proportion of the company's engineers were from Bangladesh, not only because they could be engaged cheaply but because they were well qualified at Commonwealth standards. Also, as many of Petroships' vessels were registered in Malaysia for commercial reasons, the Malaysia preference for Muslims came into play, again favouring Bangladesh.

The *Petro Ranger* was just such a ship, and I was to find that most of my officers and crew, up to 75 per cent, were Muslim. This created no problems. Conforming to Islamic law, no alcohol or pork products were carried on the ship so I was denied pork sausages and bacon—probably no bad thing as it cut down on my cholesterol intake.

Another positive of taking over a ship in dry-dock is that it gives the Captain an opportunity to screen the officers and crew at a more leisurely pace rather than when going directly into operational mode. During my briefing in the office before my first voyage, I discovered that the Captain I was taking over from had been dismissed. Apparently the money supplied to him for the direct purchase of fresh food for the ship's stores had been misused and the crew were both hungry and angry. Hungry to the point that, while in dry-dock, they had been using the shipyard's canteen to buy their own food until I arrived.

A European captain, especially an Australian, is initially viewed by South-East Asian seamen as a 'soft touch'. Within 24 hours the crew realised that this was not so in my case. Every petty complaint or request they put up I dismissed outright until I had the chance to talk to the officers and men one by one, get the feel of the past and decide how I would proceed in the future. It became clear to them that I'd dealt with South-East Asian crews before and they tended to settle down.

On my rounds I noticed that the food they were eating, other than that from the canteen, had been bought at the local market and they were cooking for themselves. The cook had been involved with the previous captain in stealing the money supplied for food by the company. Often, no proper accounting procedures governed the use of this money and the company paid little attention to it. Some captains regarded taking a cut of this money as one of their 'perks' and companies generally turn a blind eye to this practice.

The first thing I did was sack the cook and re-stock the ship with proper food. Six weeks later, after several voyages, I had to sack the replacement cook, not for dishonesty but because he couldn't cook. Third time lucky—the next cook I engaged was honest and skilled enough to cater to the culinary requirements of all the different nationalities on the ship.

Although it is necessary to be strict with a crew comprised of many nationalities to prevent disharmony, it is equally important to be fair to all. In turn, I expected fairness on their part and I believe that a simple thing like a display of honesty and insisting that the men be well fed laid a foundation of trust and made for a happy ship with myself, the officers and men bonding well in what was a small but potentially volatile community. A crew made up of many different nationalities and religions learns much about each other's customs. It has always been my practice to inspect the galley for cleanliness and, during one such inspection in the month of Ramadan, I came across the Bosun, a devout Muslim, devouring a huge fried egg sandwich. When I asked him why he was breaking his fast in such a fashion, his response would raise a smile from one of any nationality or creed: 'Sir the forbidden food is always the tastiest.'

In fact I was privileged at the end of Ramadan, near the end of a voyage in early 1998, by being invited to cut the cake at the celebration marking the end of the fasting. It was explained to me that for a non-Muslim to be so invited was a great honour and that, in a sense, I was being put in the place of the village elder who cuts the cake to signal the beginning of the celebration. I had no inkling of it then, but this informal status was to be of great importance as the drama of the hijacking of the *Petro Ranger* unfolded.

Meanwhile, tired after my long day, I showered, changed into fresh underwear and went to bed. I fell asleep almost immediately, secure behind a locked door, comfortable in the spacious bed and lulled by the motion of the ship.

2

Two knocks on the door

A noise from overhead, from the navigation bridge, wakened me with a start. A quick glance at my watch told me it was 1.30 a.m. I'd only been asleep for a few hours but sailors are used to interrupted sleep and I was alert enough. I put on a short towelling robe, having resolved to go up to the bridge to investigate. Before I reached the day room door it received a smashing blow from the outside near the lock and I heard shouting in a language I didn't immediately recognise.

My first thought was *Pirates!*

After a second heavy blow, I opened the door rather than have it smashed in and was confronted by five men wearing balaclavas. Crowding into the day room, four of them threatened me with machetes while the fifth pointed a handgun at my head. If I spoke at that point, I can't remember what I said. One of the pirates made a gesture indicating that I should put my hands together out in front of me. No resistance was possible and I complied with their instructions. He pulled off my wristwatch and wedding ring and tied my wrists together with a length of thin cord. He was an expert; the lashing was tight, and it was a sign of their preparedness that the pirates had many lengths of cord to hand for this phase of their operation.

The pirate with the handgun, later revealed as the deputy leader, spoke Indonesian-accented English. When he was satisfied that I represented no threat he demanded to know the number of crew members on board and the location of the pass key to their cabins.

Was I afraid at this point? Curiously, the answer is no. With everything happening so quickly and unexpectedly, the brain seems to freeze and the normal reactions—surprise, alarm, fear—are suspended. Plus, while it was hardly a comfort, the fact that they tied my hands indicated that I wasn't going to be killed on the spot. With the weapons they had they could certainly have done that. Subconsciously, I suppose, it came to me that I was going to survive this, at least for the time being. As in a James Bond film when the villain chains him to a bomb or stakes him out to be devoured by ants, the audience knows that escape is on the cards. Not that I had any such frivolous thoughts—I *knew* that this was deadly serious.

I'd been in dangerous situations before, especially when dealing with fires aboard ship. I'd certainly experienced fear but I'd managed to overcome it on those occasions and do what needed to be done. However, I have an absolute phobia about medical and dental procedures. If the pirates had threatened me with a dentist's drill or a syringe I would have done anything they asked and let them take the ship and cargo. Fortunately, nothing like that ever happened in this instance.

The pirates were dressed in jeans and cotton slacks and T-shirts; it was too dark to determine what they had on their feet. At 183 centimetres in my bare feet I stood taller than every one of them but, unarmed and out-numbered, I was helpless. The leader explained that I was to be conducted to each cabin and was to instruct the occupants that the ship had been attacked and they were to do exactly as they were told. If they did, no harm would come to them.

Again, strangely, as this procedure got under way, rather than feeling fear I became curious about how the assault had been mounted. How many pirates had boarded? What were their various functions? And, above all, what had happened to the officer of the watch and the lookout on the bridge?

As the officers and crew were taken from their cabins, tied up and taken away, I had no idea of their fate and became more angry than alarmed. My escort kept their razor-sharp machetes up near my head and one took to slapping the backs of my bare legs with the flat of the blade. I stopped and rounded on him; 'Drop off!' I snarled. To my surprise, he stopped and it was some comfort to know that I still had some semblance of authority even under these grim circumstances.

Whether because the crew understood more of what was being said or because they were more accustomed to seeing the results of violence, many of them were clearly terrified. The Chief Engineer, a Bangladeshi by birth but a resident of Singapore, in particular was literally catatonic with fear and the pirates had difficulty in wrenching his hands into a position in which they could be tied. Given his rank, he could have been expected to behave better.

It was later made clear to me how the attack had been carried out. Luck had been with the pirates. They had been following the ship, dead astern, for about an hour before acting. They used bamboo ladders to board the ship. The officer on watch, supposedly keeping a lookout for suspicious craft, had been apparently in the chart room tuning into his favourite Indian radio station on the navigational equipment. This was in breach of all regulations and my specific orders for the night. When surprised in the chart room by one of the pirates he had run down into the accommodation area to hide. The bridge lookout had easily been overcome by the pirates. Among the pirates were two engineers who (we found out later) had been recruited by a Singapore crewing agency under false pretences (effectively press-ganged) and were obliged to obey instructions once the enterprise had begun.[3] They had overcome the ship's engineers and taken control of the engine room.

But the deputy leader was thorough and after the cabins had been emptied he calculated, rightly, that one crew member was missing and he determined to open all doors until he was found. As we passed along the lower deck companionway towards the crew's laundry area we came upon the missing man—the officer of the watch, who had deserted his post and who was lying on his back trying to hide. When discovered he became hysterical and began screaming and thrashing about. The pirates were as surprised as I was and we halted together, which was just as well because if they hadn't stopped as I did I would have received severe wounds from the machetes still being kept close to my head. I was asked to quieten him down. I have to report that I did this by putting my foot over his mouth and exerting some pressure. He was gagged as well as bound and led away with no blood being shed.

Satisfied that the crew were all accounted for, I later learned that the pirates herded them all into my day room where they were instructed to sit with their knees raised. Their mouths were then taped and two of the pirates were detailed to guard them. The crew were mostly in their underwear, pyjamas and various states of undress and they looked a sorry lot. I was taken directly to the bridge. At this point I still didn't know how many pirates were on board or precisely what their intentions were. I knew that, as rule in these attacks, the targets were any money the ship might be carrying, the personal effects of everyone on board and any equipment or fittings of value. Bad enough, but survivable. Something about the manner of the man with the gun and the efficiency of the operation, however, gave me an inkling that something more serious was afoot.

The rounding up and securing of the crew had taken approximately an hour, so that it was still dead of night.

3

'I only want the cargo'

There were four pirates on the bridge, including the one I was to learn was the leader, who went by the name of Herman. He spoke perfect English as well as several Asian languages.

'You do not speak, Captain, except to answer our questions.'

'What if I have a question?'

'You do not ask questions.'

I was led to the pilot's chair, a high chair used by the pilot or captain when he was required to sit for long periods on the bridge manoeuvring the ship. My ankles were taped to the legs of the chair with heavy industrial tape. I was thus completely immobilised and unable to get to the VHF radio and raise an alarm. My head was pulled to one side and a knife was placed beside my neck. I was told that I'd be killed if I didn't cooperate.

Defying the instruction not to speak unless answering a question, I said, 'You're going to kill me anyway. Why should I cooperate?'

I was told that if I didn't cooperate they would kill the crew, one by one. At this point I heard screaming from where the crew was being held and I thought they were serious about the threat and had perhaps begun killing. I agreed to their terms but only if my wedding ring was returned to me.

In the context of what was happening this may sound peculiar, but my silver wedding anniversary was exactly a month away and my family was very much on my mind. Again, at a subconscious level, I suppose I felt that recovering my wedding ring would connect me in some way with my loved ones in the midst of this nightmare.

Linguistic problems arose. Apparently they were more familiar with the term 'wedding band' than 'wedding ring' and it took a few minutes to sort this out. They demanded to know who had taken my ring and was told it was the man who had tied my hands. Within two or three minutes I felt rough hands on mine and when the ring was back in place on the correct finger I began to cooperate.

Although I imagine that a heart and pulse monitor would have shown that I was under considerable stress, my conscious reactions were still more of curiosity than fear. I noted that the result of maintaining outward calm myself was to make the pirates less agitated and aggressive. But not less menacing. Herman, balaclava-masked, approached and hissed that he knew that I had a wife and two daughters and where they lived and could guarantee that harm would befall them if I didn't cooperate fully.

The reason why the pirates did not kill me on the spot and negotiated for my help was that they were ignorant of how to operate the ship's navigational equipment. I later learned that this was the largest and most modern vessel they had hijacked, and they weren't able to cope with its advanced technology. Herman explained that they didn't know how to change from automatic pilot to manual steering. I was cut loose from the chair and the tape torn from my legs (to this day I have never been able to understand how women volunteer to have their legs waxed) and, still with my hands tied and weapons bristling around me, I was taken to the steering column and had to explain the controls to the pirate leader. The Third Engineer was under the control of the pirates and I had to instruct him by telephone to obey my orders however unusual. This was necessary because the ship was then running on heavy fuel, not the usual arrangement for this manoeuvre. Only small movements were needed at the controls and I was able to demonstrate the workings with my wrists tied.

As instructed, I slowed the ship down and brought it around onto a course clear of other shipping, also putting the pirates' boat, which I then discovered was tied up alongside the ship, on the lee, or protected side. I learned later that they had put out from the Malyasian coast, about 40 kilometres distant, to intercept the *Petro Ranger*.[4] This done, I was returned to the pilot's chair and had my legs taped to it again. My hands were tied throughout.

At this point I thought I had served my purpose and that the pirates would throw me overboard taped to the chair. Although I am a Christian who attends church fairly regularly, religious matters are not usually uppermost in my mind. At that time, however, I had long, silent conversations with God, and made a kind of pledge that if I survived the ordeal I would pay a special visit to my local church to give thanks.

Again, there was a sort of detachment from what was actually happening. I remember thinking that if they were going to knife me I'd rather be stabbed in the heart than have my throat cut. From films I'd seen the former method looked quicker than the latter. I even had a sort of fantasy about requesting this if given the chance—like the Mexican bandit tied to the post and being given the option of the blindfold. My thoughts were much focused on my wife and daughters and the distress they would feel if things turned out badly. Strangely enough, when thinking of my daughters,

I could only recall the pet names we'd had for them as children, not their actual names. A mind under stress plays odd tricks.

These considerations were interrupted when all the main deck lights were switched on and the Bosun was marched out with a knife at his throat and made to operate the ship's crane. It was already clear that this was no smash-and-grab raid; now the pirates arranged to have their boat hoisted on board.

Herman then told me, 'I only want the cargo, not the ship.' My mind was thrown into further confusion as this was the first time I had ever heard of, not to say encountered, the idea of stealing the ship and I didn't realise the full implications, but I was aware that what he'd said didn't guarantee our survival. For the moment, I was racking my brains to come up with a way of getting free of the chair were I thrown over-board. This was a waste of effort really, because in that event chair and man would have been drawn into the propeller and shredded.

As others who have survived life and death situations have noted, there is often a comical note struck in the proceedings. And so it was for me as the pirates struggled to lift their boat with equipment only geared to a 2.5 tonne load. Meanwhile, taped ignominiously to a chair with a knife at my throat and a machete to my groin, watching the activities on deck, I suddenly had a Marlboro cigarette placed in my mouth and lit for me. That was the best cigarette I've ever smoked. As a result of a medical problem some time before, I had stopped smoking and had been tobacco-free for sixteen months before the attack. But I eagerly smoked that cigarette and was immediately hooked again, enjoying it more than ever. Smoking might be bad for your health but, then again, so are pirates.

It took perhaps an hour to get the boat on board and then the lights were switched off and the crane rehoused. With dawn still some time away, I was released from the chair and instructed to get the ship back onto full sea speed and reset the autopilot to our original course. As long as I live I will never forget that course: 018 degrees true.

Between cigarettes they fed me orange juice, which took me utterly by surprise as I didn't expect any such consideration. It was a very humid night and I was drenched with sweat and the orange juice which had been spilled down my chin and front by the pirate but, given the seriousness of my situation, I barely noticed it. Then I had to give the leader basic instruction in how to operate our radar and GPS[5] and repeatedly go over how to use the manual and automatic steering. The whole time this was going on we were assailed by the irritating sound of the Indian music the officer of the watch had tuned into.

'How do you turn that off?' the leader eventually asked me. I flipped the switch.

Then I had to lie on the deck with one pirate guarding me until the leader felt confident at the controls. He wasn't exactly a brilliant student, but he seemed competent enough.

Then it was down to my cabin where the crew were still tied up but with the tape taken from their mouths. To a man they were in a state of shock. I was thrown onto my bed and very shortly fell asleep, either from exhaustion or shock or a combination of both. It was still dark.

4

Held hostage

When I woke up, with no idea of how long I'd been asleep, the scene around me was like a war zone. My accommodation had been totally ransacked and my personal belongings and the ship's papers strewn everywhere. I could see into the day room through my bedroom door; the crew were all tied at the wrists as I was and the pirates had discovered a blue movie belonging to one of the crew and several of them were watching it on my VCR. One pirate, wielding a machete and swigging from a can of soft drink, was actually standing on a crew man while another was going through my fridge for food.

When the man with the machete and soft drink saw that I was awake he approached and, using one of the crew as an interpreter, demanded the combination of the ship's safe. I explained that the lock on the safe wasn't working and that the money he was after—about two thousand dollars, what was left of the amount I'd been given to buy fresh food in Singapore—was in an envelope in a compartment of my attaché case. This made him angry; he grabbed the money and struck me on the head with the handle of his machete, knocking me out.

It was around midday when I came to. One of the crew still had his Casio watch which the pirates had evidently thought too cheap to bother stealing. After about an hour I was taken to the officers' mess room, a spacious room, large enough to contain two tables with seating for twelve or so. The room had been cleared and the mattresses from the crew's and officers' bunks had been laid on the floor. The door to the galley had been lashed shut so that the only entry was through the one forward door. This was to be our prison.

I was given the privilege of selecting the mattress of my choice and then the rest of the crew were brought down (all except the Third Engineer, who was kept in the engine room control area) and distributed themselves around the space. It was cramped and when moving around one had to be careful not to step on another person. Some of the crew members were unable to sleep at all because they were terrified that the pirates would massacre them if they did. Others slept only when they were exhausted.

Now that they were fully in control of the ship and all personnel, the pirates appeared to relax somewhat. They took off their balaclavas, which must have been uncomfortable in the heat, and some of their aggression fell away. I realised that they must have been keyed up and fearful during the seizure of the ship in case things went wrong and they were now feeling some relief that the most dangerous part of the operation was over.

At four o'clock each crew member, under guard, was allowed to shower. I was honoured; I had two guards but was allowed to use my own bathroom and get a change of clothes. It was a relief to get out of my sweaty and orange juice-soaked robe and underwear and into clean things. By this time certain members of the crew had exchanged a few words with the pirates and we learned that most of them were Indonesians.

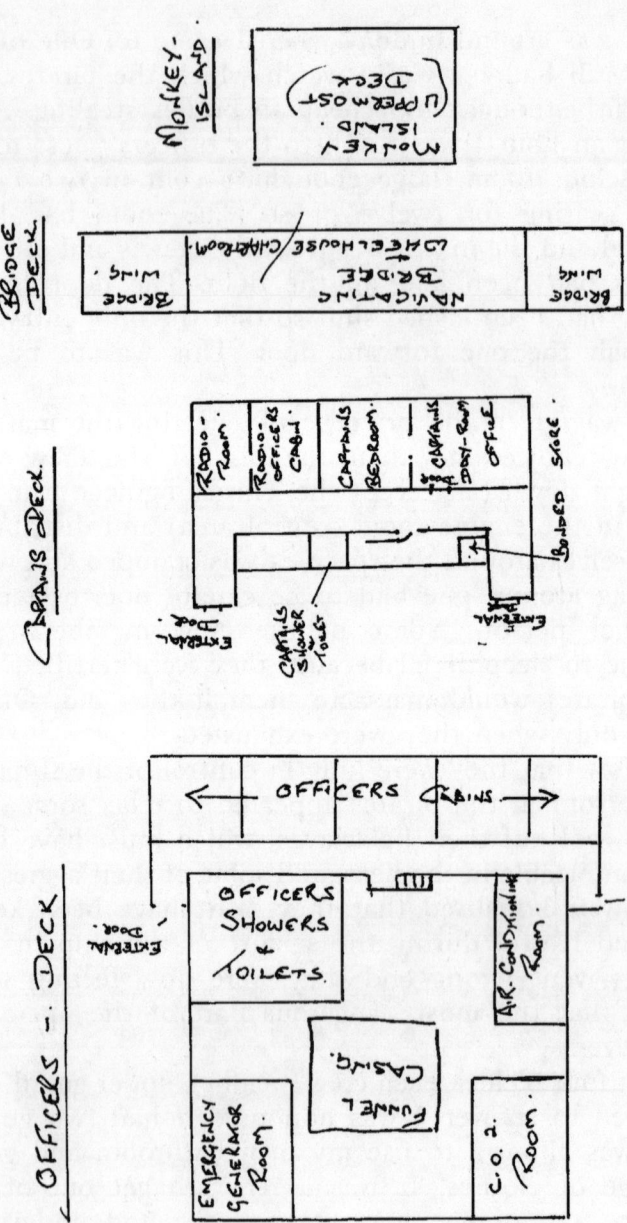

2. The author's plan of the layout of the
   MT *Petro Ranger*.

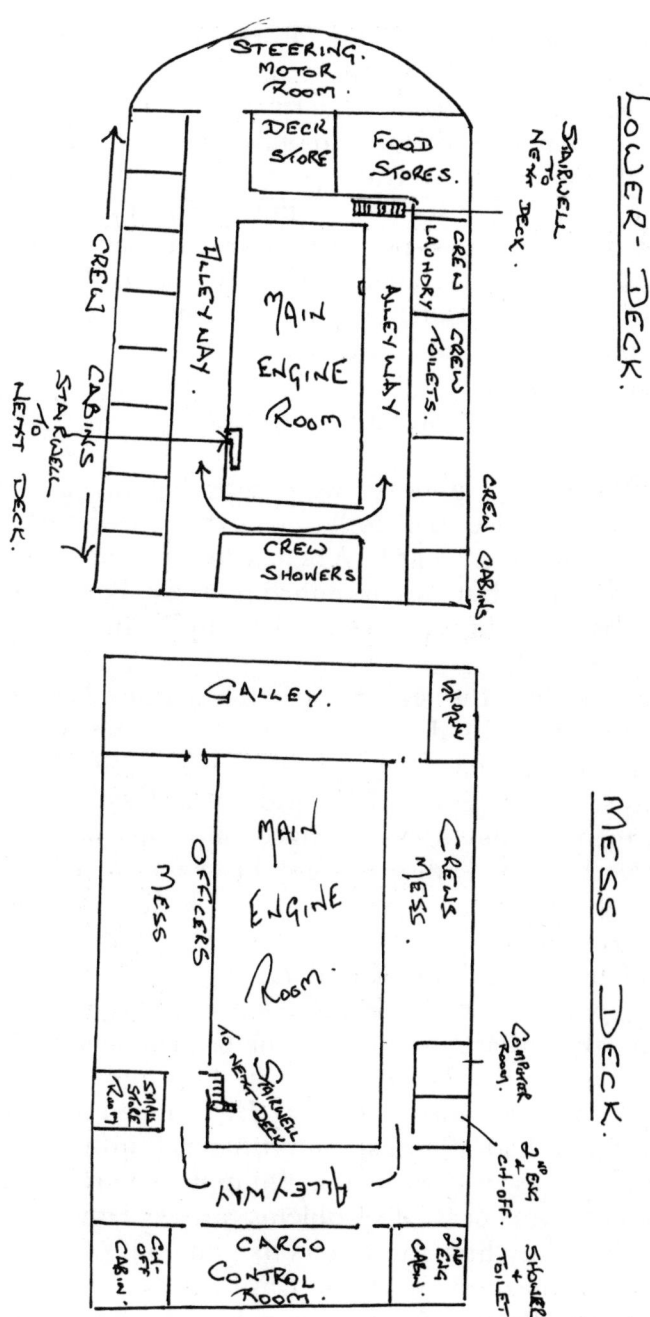

Using the Bosun and Chief Officer as interpreters, I arranged a meeting with the pirate leader.

At around five o'clock Herman and I met in my day room where a certain amount of order had been restored. We spoke over a cup of coffee and, strangely enough, it was almost like two businessmen meeting to discuss a transaction—not exactly friendly, but cordial.

I said, 'I want my cook to have access to the galley between 6.00 a.m. and 1.00 p.m. and between 3.00 p.m. and 6.00 p.m. each day to prepare meals.'

'Agreed, Captain.'

'His hands will have to be freed.'

A nod.

Daily showering times were agreed upon and the crew were to use the toilets on the mess deck as needed, but under guard. When urinating their hands remained tied, but when relieving their bowels one wrist was freed but they were tied up again immediately afterwards.

By this time the leader's general attitude had softened and I realised that he wanted some sort of recognition for what he had achieved. He could hardly broadcast his success to the world but at least he could boast to me about how he seized my ship.

'I work for a syndicate, Captain,' he said. 'It is run like any other large corporation with permanent employees, some of ten years' standing, and a capital base of many millions of dollars.'

I expressed polite interest and he went on to explain that there were four main members of the syndicate: one in Jakarta, one in Singapore, one in Hong Kong and one in China. He claimed that the organisation had political and financial influence in these places as well as in the Philippines which could be brought to bear if problems arose. Funds were available to buy him and others like him out of trouble.

'And in the present case?' I asked.

'Thoroughly researched,' he said. 'We knew about

your cargo weeks beforehand and exactly when the pilot would depart your ship and what your position would be when we were ready to move. Also that the ship carries no arms.'

Then, to my astonishment, he added that the syndicate had access to all phases of Petroships' operations and that knowledge had greatly assisted them in their planning. In addition, he said that he had prior information about my two daughters and, since there was nothing on record about my family anywhere on the ship, I believed him.

Since he knew so much about me I ventured to ask him about himself. He said that he was 49 years of age and held Indonesian master mariner's papers. His account of how he got into piracy spoke volumes about the nature of things in South-East Asia. He said that in his younger days ethnic Chinese shipowners in Indonesia hired him to take their ships out to sea and sink them so that they could collect the insurance. He felt that he wasn't being paid enough for the risks and money involved and so he progressed to piracy where the returns were much greater. He was single with no family and his activities financed a lifestyle he greatly enjoyed: first-class world travel and accommodation in five-star hotels. Other attractions he left to my imagination.

This might sound chatty but in fact serious instructions were being issued. He stressed that the crew were not to engage in conversation with his men and that I was to tell them so. He repeated that all he wanted was the cargo and the services of the crew were needed for the work of transferring the fuel to other tankers. The details of this would be discussed nearer the time.

'But, Captain, anyone who fails to cooperate will be killed. Do you understand?'

I said I understood. He then said I should reassure the crew that once the cargo was transferred they would be released and that the ship would be allowed to return to Singapore. No harm would come to them. By implication, this applied to me as well but I simply did not believe him. I was sure that he had told me far too much about the syndicate to allow me to live.

He had to return to the bridge and I was escorted back to the mess room. And so ended one of the strangest days of my life. I had started out as the master of a ship and ended up as a hostage aboard her; but, for the present, I was still alive and my crew were unhurt.

5

Machine-guns and a movie

On the 18th the routine that was to dominate our lives for the next ten days was established. We were kept under guard in the mess room, three pirates taking turns at six-hour watches. The lights were kept on 24 hours a day and our wrists were kept bound. But the pirates did us no harm and I later learned that the leader had severely castigated the one who had hit me. The leader feared that his action might either incite the crew to rebel against them or terrify them still more, causing them to wonder what might happen to them and make their behaviour less predictable. So the pirate who had knocked me out was ordered to publicly apologise to me through the Chief Officer, who acted as interpreter. This didn't fool anyone but it showed what a shrewd operator the leader was. He needed the crew to cooperate without too much duress. None of this should be taken to mean that the pirates were in any way 'nice guys'. They were ruthless criminals with nothing romantic about them.

This brings me to the important matter of food. Obviously, in South-East Asia many people do not get enough food and the opportunity to get good food and plenty of it is highly valued. The Indonesian cook aboard the *Petro Ranger* was excellent at his job and

I stressed that the pirates were to get food of the same quality and in the same quantity as the crew. This was a form of reverse psychology on my part. I wanted to lull the pirates into a false sense of security (always having in mind the idea of escaping). The good food was appreciated by the pirates and helped to make them better disposed towards us. They also seemed to want to communicate more with the crew. And so, in my own way, I'd begun to fight back.

The officers and crew ate in the crew's mess room three times daily but only half of the number at any one time. I couldn't eat the same highly spiced food and I instructed the cook to reserve the bread supply and the fresh fruit for me. The others were getting their vitamins and minerals in the vegetables. I lived on eggs, bread, frozen pizzas and fruit, eating alone in the officers' mess room. Although the voyage had been scheduled to last only two days we had food supplies for ten or more. The supply of juice soon ran out but we had plenty of tea and coffee and reconstituted milk.

No significant contact was taking place between the pirates and the crew as the latter were still mostly in a state of holy terror. When in the shower in my bathroom, I could see out of the toilet portholes directly at the funnel and I saw that the lower half of it had been painted red, leaving the upper half blue. So a process of disguising the ship was under way. The pirates covered all portholes and windows on the mess deck with brown paper, which they taped into place and painted over so that nothing occurring outside could be seen. As the cargo control room, the Chief Officer's and Second Engineer's cabins were on this deck, their windows and portholes were blacked out.

At 2.00 p.m. the Radio Officer was taken to the communications room to tune the ship's single-band radio to the frequency that would enable Herman to contact his principal in China. After doing this he was returned to the mess room but not before he had observed something alarming: two machine-guns being kept in the radio room. So the means of killing the lot of us were at hand.

The ropes around our wrists were beginning to chafe and, as open sores are dangerous in the tropics, I requested a further meeting with the leader to see if there was some other way of tying our wrists. Again, over cigarettes and coffee, the meeting was amicable and it was agreed that a different method would be found.

'We are running short of tobacco, Captain,' the leader said.

This shortage had begun to affect the crew and myself as well, so I showed the pirates where the ship's supply of bonded cigarettes was kept. All smokers on board quickly went from a famine to a feast, cigarette-wise, thus increasing the pirates' feelings of goodwill.

The leader also told me that he'd require the assistance of my Chief Officer and Bosun the next day to instruct his men on how to line up the cargo valves on deck and in the pump room ready for the transfer of the fuel to other tankers, whenever that might be.

The heartlessness and cruelty of the pirates was demonstrated when they held a machete to the throat of the hapless officer who had neglected his post and tried to hide after the attack and forced him to sing a song, supposedly for our entertainment. It was a sad and demeaning sight and I found it difficult to know where to look.

During that day the six junior members of the pirate gang looted the cabins, taking all the valuables and money they could find. They decided that the crew had better clothes than theirs so they took them and the crew's toiletries. They also had the crew's VCR and their store of videos at their disposal and made use of them constantly. The only entertainment we had in the mess room was, rather aptly, a copy of the film *Titanic*.[6] I watched it so often over the next ten days that I'm sure I couldn't bear to see it again. So our second day as hostages ended peacefully but in great discomfort. It's no easy matter to sleep with your wrists tied. I slept flat on my stomach with my hands held out above my head but I wouldn't say I slept well.

Over the next two days the atmosphere became more relaxed and I decided to encourage those members of the crew who had compatriots amongst the pirates—Malaysians and Indonesians—to talk with them and find out what they could about them. This was in defiance of Herman's order but it seemed worth the risk and the crew were gradually becoming less frightened and willing to do something that was in their own interest. By this means I discovered that the pirates all carried forged Indonesian passports but only seven of them were actually Indonesians. By their dialects and accents the crew worked out that three were Malaysian and two were Thais. Herman was Indonesian as was his deputy and also another pair who I guessed were executioners. These four always worked together and were the only ones with access to the firearms and the navigating bridge and radio room. The other six, whom I thought of as simply thugs, did whatever they were told. One of the Malaysians, I discovered, had been released from jail in Johore just three days before attacking the ship. The two pirate engineers never left the control room of the engine room. Their meals were brought in to them and a mattress was commandeered for them to sleep on.

On the 19th the pirates came up with another method of keeping us secure. They took spare 'O' rings (round, thick rubber seals) from the engine room store, placed them round our hands and taped the rings together with industrial tape, making their own brand of handcuffs. This was more comfortable than being tied with rope but it became a chore for the pirates to have to cut and retape when we moved our bowels and showered. Eventually we were able to work our hands free of the rings and we did so for periods of time but took care not to let the pirates see us doing it.

By this time the overcrowded mess room was in a bad state and I insisted to the pirates that it had to be swept and cleaned. I was afraid that so many men confined in a space would lead to sickness unless the room was kept reasonably clean and hygienic. The same applied to the cabins where the guards were spending their time. Using the Chief Officer as an interpreter I got him to ask one of the guards to make this clear to the leader.

'No problem, no problem,' the guard said when he returned.

So the mess room and the cabins were cleaned thoroughly, the mattresses aired and the area washed down with disinfectant.

All in all the pirates became more obliging, the younger ones even apologising for the rough handling we'd received initially. When taken to my quarters to shower, I noticed that my attaché case had been broken open and rifled but I discovered that all my Department of Transport qualifications had been left undisturbed in my bedroom. I asked by gesture to be allowed to take them down to the mess room with me and to my surprise this was accepted. Presumably this man, being uneducated and unable to speak or read English, didn't appreciate the importance of the papers. My passport was among these papers. I put them in my attaché case and had a close watch on the case kept from that time on. The possession of those documents was later to be vitally important.

The following morning the leader had me brought to my cabin, which he was using, for a meeting. Before leaving Singapore I had written on the whiteboard near my desk in big letters '23RD APRIL—FLIGHT QF 52—DEP. 1940 ARR. BRISBANE 0450/24TH'. Herman must have been curious about this because he asked me hesitantly what it meant. I explained that it was the flight I'd been due to catch to return home. I had trouble preventing myself from bursting out laughing as with his voice dripping with sincerity, he said he wished I could send a telex to advise that I'd be delayed somewhat, but under the circumstances . . . I assured him that I realised his predicament and understood. We both should have been nominated for Oscars.

As before, we talked over coffee and cigarettes but on this occasion it was not as amicable as previously. He told me that his principal in China wanted us all killed before the ship entered Chinese waters. (It was already apparent to me from what I could gather about our course based on what I could see from my unblacked-out window in my shower recess and the nature of the weather that China was our destination.) But he had advised that we were needed to carry out the transfer of the cargo, which was the whole object of the operation. So the people in China had agreed to keep us alive.

For how long? I wondered. But I didn't ask.

This information strengthened my resolve that, when the appropriate time came and an opportunity presented itself, we would have to make a break and try to overrun the pirates. At the time I had no idea of how to achieve this and I strongly felt the lack of another European to discuss the matter with and come up with a plan. Two heads are usually better than one and I would have been glad of someone else whose thinking ran along the same lines to confer with. But for the moment I had to keep these thoughts to myself.

Herman gave directions that the Chief Officer and the Bosun would be required to go out onto the main deck and to the pump room that afternoon to commence lining up the valves and the pumps to discharge the fuel into other tankers.

'There must be no mistakes, Captain. No slip-ups,

or I will have members of the crew killed on the spot as an example.'

I was sure he meant it and, as this was not the time to offer any resistance, I gave instructions that his orders were to be closely followed. The arrangement was that all the valves that had to be opened and shut in the transfer operation were to be clearly marked so that only the pirates would be on deck when this was going on. Not easy to arrange but it was done. By this time the six youngest pirates were on reasonably friendly terms with some of the crew and were communicating freely as long as the leaders were not around. They were satisfied that the preparations of the valves and pumps had been done properly and that nothing clandestine had taken place.

All this proved to me was the pirates were out of their depth when it came to using our automated cargo system. This clearly was of benefit to us as, in a sense, we had become indispensable as long as the ship carried its cargo.

6

The search

With a lot of blank time to fill, my thoughts were very much with my family, knowing how worried they would be when news of our plight broke. However, I had no idea of how or when that might happen. In fact a nightmarish period began for my wife, Denise, and my daughters, Linda and Wendy, when, at 2.45 p.m. on Monday 20 April, Captain Johnny Liew, Petroships' Marine Superintendent in Singapore, phoned Denise at our home in the Queensland Gold Coast hinterland, to tell her that the *Petro Ranger* had disappeared.

According to Captain Liew nothing had been heard from the ship for more than 24 hours and that although every means possible had been tried no contact could be made. Denise asked about the weather conditions and was told of clear skies and a calm sea. Captain Liew ended this conversation by saying that all appropriate authorities had been informed and the suspicion was that the ship had been taken by pirates and its appearance and registration changed. It was not until the next day that Denise was told that a telex sent from the ship at about noon on the 17th advising of her position and other routine navigational details was the last that had been heard from the ship.

Denise phoned Linda at work in Brisbane, who drove home immediately, and Wendy at the Edinburgh RAAF base where she was stationed. Wendy undertook to make enquiries. Denise also contacted her sister, various friends and the minister of our local church. Repeated attempts to learn more by telephone from Petroships in Singapore failed.

This initial phone call from Petroships on the 20th to Denise saying I had been missing for over 24 hours (they elected not to mention I had in fact been missing for three days) was to set in motion a chain of events no one could have predicted, least of all Petroships. My older daughter, an officer in the RAAF, was at that time attached to the Air Commodore's staff, the Air Commodore being the Commander of the Maritime Patrol Group. Wendy was obviously shocked and distressed and when the Commodore found out why, he immediately contacted Australia's Defence Adviser in the Australian High Commission in Singapore and explained the situation. The adviser at once contacted Petroships for a description of the *Petro Ranger* and forwarded this information to the commanding officer at RAAF Butterworth in Malaysia.

Fortunately, an Orion aircraft (a maritime surveillance plane) was in South-East Asia on international commitments and the next day it overflew all known shipping lanes that the ship could have taken. But by that time it was too late.[7]

On Tuesday 21 April, probably around the time Herman was telling me of the stay in our execution, Denise phoned the Department of Foreign Affairs and Trade (DFAT) in Canberra and was told to contact the Australian Maritime Safety Authority (AMSA). She did this and learned that they knew nothing of the matter. She supplied the scanty information she had and AMSA got busy. Within a few hours AMSA phoned to tell Denise that the Singapore Director of Marine Operations had issued a Navigation Warning Broadcast to the effect that the MT *Petro Ranger* was believed to have been taken by pirates. All ships and aircraft in the vicinity were requested to be on the lookout and report if the vessel was sighted. This warning was issued at 9.00 a.m. Singapore time on 21 April.

Denise contacted Petroships and requested them to advise the Australian High Commission in Singapore of the disappearance of an Australian national. The company had not done this, nor did they until the 22nd.

On Tuesday 21 April, Jim Harper, head of the DFAT's search division, phoned Denise to tell her that he would be her contact on the case. He said that he had only heard of the matter an hour earlier but would be contacting all Australian embassies and consulates in South-East Asia advising them that a ship was missing with an Australian national on board and requesting them to render all assistance if it was found.

Wires were sent on the following day by DFAT to consulates and embassies and DFAT also advised Denise on what to do if the media picked up the story. That evening Captain Liew phoned with the news that Honolulu's Pacific Rescue Coordination Centre may have had a contact and the American Embassy was informed. Later, it was confirmed that this contact was false.

Thursday 23 April was a nerve-rackingly empty day for Denise until 5.00 p.m. when Jim Harper rang to say that he had made contact with all relevant authorities but as yet there was no news. He suggested that the ship may have been taken to the Philippines, Indonesia or Thailand as had happened to other vessels. The only positive aspect of this was that in previous cases only the cargo was taken and the crews had been released unharmed.

This was the day I *should* have been leaving for home and Denise and my daughters felt the impact of this very strongly. They weren't getting much sleep

AN ACT OF PIRACY

460 Alexandra Road
#25-04 PSA Building
Singapore 119963

Telephone : 273 1122
Telex : RS 24176
Fax : 273 2200

Date: 22 April 1998

To :
    Defense Advisor
    Australian High Commission
    Singapore

Fax :

TOP URGENT

Dear Sir,

Re : M.T. Petro Ranger – Australian Master on board

We wish to inform you that we have lost communications with the M.T. Petro Ranger, a Malaysian registered vessel under our management, since Friday ~~19~~ April 1998. The Master on board is an Australian citizen and his details are as follows:

17th

Captain Kenneth John Blyth
Passport No.

Next-of-Kin : Mrs Denise Clare Blyth
Relationship: Wife

Queensland Australia

Tel:

Currently we have not received any information regarding the vessel yet. We seek your assistance to help us locate the vessel.

Thank you.

Capt. Johnny Liew
Marine Superintendent

3. Edited copy of the fax dated 22 April 1998 in which Petroships erroneously date their loss of contact with the *Petro Ranger* at 19 April 1998.

and, like the friends they'd notified, they felt numb. Although she wouldn't call herself a believer in telepathy, Denise had a strong feeling that I wasn't dead. Many years before she'd had a sense that I was in trouble and had phoned the ship I was on, which happened to be in Adelaide. I answered the phone and she said, 'What's wrong?'

There was indeed a problem of some kind and I said, 'How did you know anything was wrong?'

'I just knew,' she said.

Similarly she 'just knew' that I wasn't dead, but that still left a great deal to worry about.

The next day, when Denise should have been collecting me at the airport bright and early, she wandered about the house feeling empty and helpless. She got the usual 'no news' phone call from DFAT and, desperate to do something, she phoned a colleague of mine in Singapore. He was shocked at the news because there had been no reports about the disappearance of the ship in the local media. He undertook to make enquiries, phoned back with another number for her to ring, supposedly a useful contact. Nothing came of this except that she learned that the Australian High Commission in Singapore had the matter at the top of its priority list. Otherwise there was nothing new.

By this time it was a week since I'd been heard from. Denise packed a small suitcase and collected up her passport and other paperwork so that she'd be ready to fly out at a moment's notice *when* (and she was still sure it would be when) I was located. She and the girls and friends could scarcely comprehend that piracy was still going on at the end of the twentieth century. Surely it was a thing of the distant past. They looked at a large atlas we kept at home and were faced with the fact that there were thousands of islands dotted around the area. Indonesia consists of more than 3000 inhabited islands; there are over 400 in the Philippines. Where do you begin to look?

On Saturday 25 April, Denise attended the Anzac Day ceremony, commemorating the landing of Anzac troops at Gallipoli in 1915, at Coomera and was reduced to tears.

Captain Liew phoned and told Denise that close contact was being kept with all South-East Asian embassies, particularly in Malaysia. There was no hard news but there was a vague, unconfirmed report that a ship that *may* have been the *Petro Ranger* had been seen heading for the Philippines.

A bizarre note is sounded at this point. Petroships claimed that this report, no stronger than a rumour, derived from two anonymous satellite telephone calls. In the first place, it is impossible to make an anonymous satellite phone call. All such calls, strangely enough, have to be paid for in Belgian francs, and are closely monitored. In fact, Petroships had consulted a clairvoyant about the disappearance of their vessel and the clairvoyant had come up with the Philippines suggestion. This was the true source of this red herring.

On Sunday Denise went to church and was comforted by the congregation. Denise and my daughters were fortunate in that the media had not got wind of the story until that Sunday, by which time they'd come to terms with the situation to some extent. Once the story broke they were under constant media harassment. The story was on Sydney radio the night before and on the BBC world news in the morning. Channel 7 turned up at the front door at 3.00 p.m. and from then on there were phone calls and knocks on the door throughout the day and continuing almost until midnight.

Following the DFAT advice, they maintained a strict 'no comment' policy, insisting that no photographs would be given out and asking that their privacy be respected. Some chance. The members of the media

460 Alexandra Road
#25-04 PSA Building
Singapore 119963

Telephone : 273 1122
Telex : RS 24176
Fax : 273 2200

Date: 30 April 1998

To :

Defense Advisor
Australian High Commission
Singapore

Fax :

PRIVATE AND CONFIDENTIAL

Dear Sir,

RE: PETRO RANGER MISSING

We enclose herewith sketches made by our clairvoyant on the 28th April 1998 about 0030 hours for your information. Kindly take note some of the visions may be symbolic in nature. The funnel part closely resembles one of the special feature of the ship although I have not told her about it.

Thank you and best regards.

Capt. Johnny Liew
Marine Superintendent

4. The clairvoyant hired by Petroships supplied some surprisingly accurate sketches and information, which can be seen on the following pages.

behaved more or less as in the ABC comedy series 'Frontline'. Privacy was not a word in their vocabulary. Denise screened all calls on the answering machine but it was frustrating to have the line so busy when she wanted it clear hoping for the call that would set her mind at rest. Worst of all were the calls in the early hours when the journalists were hoping to catch my family off guard and trick them into giving a phone

AN ACT OF PIRACY

J. nny Liew - Capt - Petro Ships 2731122

Message taken 10.10am 24/4

Clairvoyant called at midnight 23/4. Crew seem to be in better health. 1 or 2 weak.
Captain seems better. Chief Officer better. Some crew and engineers seem to have a little
more energy than others so may be working.

Ship:
Seems more in motion - same area 5° north 110 ° east. Intermittent vibrations - like bus
stopping and starting - sort of revving. Had a glimpse of a guy. Looks like a Cambodian -
small build - thick frizzy hair, shoulder length. Wearing black singlet and brown pants.
Walking up and down inside cubicle - it has a shelf in front and two square pillars, one
right and one left.

His opinion:
We can infer ship is moving around same area - guy is probably on navigating bridge.
Thought it was interesting that the clairvoyant knows nothing about ships but from what
she describes it seems like bridge.

The Malaysian Embassy in Hanoi cantacted Capt Liew last night to advise him that they
were going to contact the Vietnamese Government to see if they can patrol the area.

The Ministry of Foreign Affairs KL called asking for information. Capt Liew asked them
to please contact the Australian High Commissions in Kl and Sing.

Capt Liew will contact Ministry of Foreign Affairs in KL today requesting them to advice
embassies in Bangkok, Phnom Penh, Manila and Jakarta of situation.

interview. This was cruel, given that calls at night could
reasonably be expected to relay bad news.

Initial media reports on the case were a mixture of
fact and fantasy. Denise began collecting clippings from
day one and, in retrospect, they make interesting reading. A report in *The Australian* of 27 April is relatively
sober and accurate as far as it goes although it follows
the chronology as laid out by Petroships which, as will be
discussed later, is seriously flawed. The *Petro Ranger* was
described as being 'on charter' to a Vietnamese company
which owned the cargo. A company named Enerfrate was
given as the 'charter agent' of the ship and its spokesman
claimed that it had sought the help of the RAAF and the
navies of Thailand, Vietnam and the Philippines.

This plain account was not good enough, however,
for the *Gold Coast Bulletin*, which ran a long article,

PETRO-PIRATES

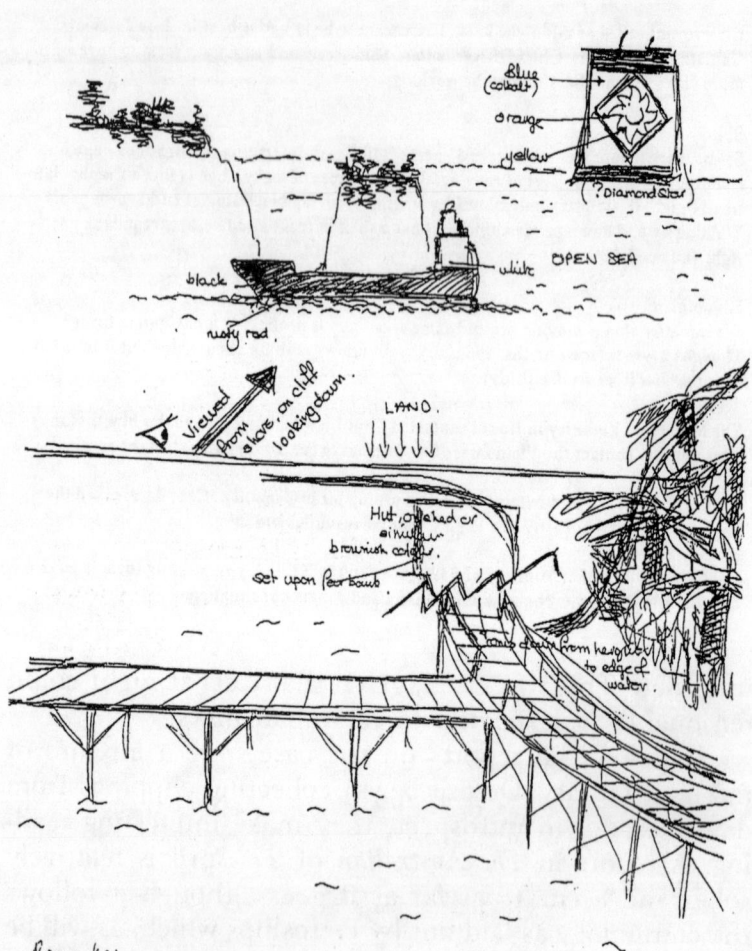

Blue (cobalt)

orange

yellow

? Diamond Star

OPEN SEA

white

black

rusty red.

Viewed from above, on cliff looking down

LAND

↓ ↓ ↓ ↓ ↓

Hut, on shed or similar brownish colour.

set upon fire bomb

Land drops from here(?) to edge of water.

<u>Remarks:</u>

1) Vision on 28/April 1998 about 0030hrs.

2) Felt vessel around Caban/Lubang Is. (13° 45'N 120° 15'E)

3) The island on the Land side felt quite steep running into the sea.

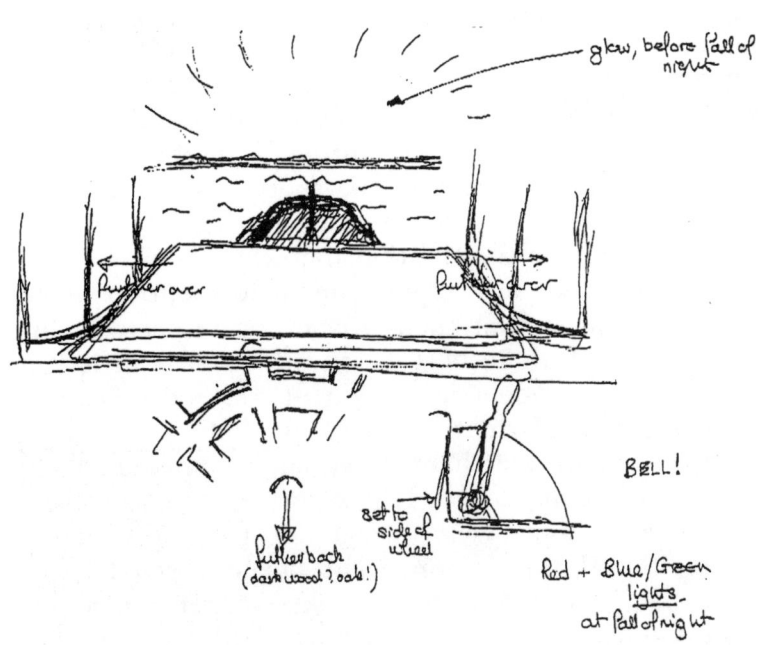

illustrated by a swashbuckling scene, that stressed the sensational: 'The buccaneers have traded in their cutlasses and now brandish assault rifles equipped with night vision optics.' This article ran through some of the bloodier acts of piracy in recent times with no strict regard to geography. In an accompanying piece, it referred to me as 'our Captain Blyth' and contained some misinformation: a reported sighting of the *Petro Ranger* in Philippine waters, between the south-western island of Palawan and north of Sabah, and naming Petroships as the 'agent' of the vessel rather than the owner.

All of these early reports included mention of my family's request that their privacy be respected while the press did their best to invade it. An article of 2 May in the Adelaide edition of *The Australian* had dug up some information on me, including my service in the British merchant navy and employment by various oil companies. The report quoted a former shipmate of mine (who asked not to be named) as saying that I was 'a somewhat fiery-tempered Scotsman, but a very competent tanker officer and a very close family man'. The latter part of this statement is true enough, about the rest others would have to judge.

This article ventured further than others in speculating what might have happened in the South China Sea. The result was an odd mixture of accuracy and guesswork:

> The pirates most probably struck late at night from behind, taking the crew by surprise. The fuel would have been transferred to another ship and sold on the black market with fake papers. By now the pirates would have repainted the ship and given it a new name, moving it at night away from shipping lanes.

That was pretty close to what happened, but the estimate of the force needed to do the job was wildly astray: 'Piracy experts say as few as two armed men could have overrun the unarmed crew . . .'

Looking through Denise's collection of clippings, it's almost amusing to see how the press struggled to get accurate information, sometimes succeeding, sometimes not. Accounts of the involvement of US and Australian naval vessels and the Philippines coast guard were more or less correct, but the report that an RAAF C–130 Hercules was searching the area was quite wrong. In fact, as noted, an Orion aircraft, in the locality on international commitments, had been requested by the RAAF to keep a lookout for the ship while pursuing its other duties.

Wednesday 29 April was an especially trying day for Denise as it was my 53rd birthday. She kept busy doing routine chores and expended some energy in mowing the grass on our large block. DFAT advised that the Malaysian High Commissioner had been called in to the department to report on what that country was doing. Whips were being cracked but there was still no news and it was a matter of waiting and waiting.

Although her main concern was my welfare, Denise could not help turning over certain questions in her mind: why had Petroships delayed so long in reporting the ship missing? Why were spokesmen for the company attempting, in statements to the media, to disclaim ownership of the vessel? Why was the Singaporean government apparently so inactive?

7

Unloading the cargo

On 22 April, the sixth day after the attack, there was a marked change in the pirates' attitude and manner. They appeared edgy and nervous. Muslim prayer mats and head coverings appeared and there were regular calls to prayers. I asked the Bosun to enquire into all this and he reported that the younger members of the gang (the ones I thought of as 'the thugs') were becoming apprehensive about the next phase of the operation and feared that all might not go well for them. My impression was that they feared they might be dispensed with and their places taken by thugs from the Chinese end of the syndicate. I told the Bosun to get the crew to encourage these feelings among the six young pirates, to tell them stories about what the Chinese would do to them if they were taken.

I felt a lack of trust seeping in between the thugs and the four senior pirates, so it was a case of always being on the alert, watching the thugs' body language, whether happy or depressed, cocky or apprehensive. I had a plan to get them on side or at least neutralise them. Then I thought that if I and a couple of the more reliable types among the crew could get hold of a gun we might be able to get on top of the other pirates. It might have worked but there would almost certainly have been casualties.

At lunch, Herman summoned me to my cabin and told me he expected to rendezvous with two tankers—a 2000-tonne vessel and one of 4000 tonnes—at approximately five o'clock that afternoon. He wanted to discharge into both tankers simultaneously and asked if this was possible. I told him that it was if one tanker was brought alongside to port and the other to starboard. During the discharge we were to be locked in the mess room and none of us was to see the tankers or their crews. These were *his* instructions and for a very good reason—he claimed that armed Chinese naval personnel were aboard these tankers, but they may have been members of the Chinese equivalent of the Federal Police, the Public Security Bureau (PSB). Herman was very firm on this point: any member of my crew suspected of sighting the tankers or their crew would be killed. With this kind of security in force, it was easy now to understand the apprehension of some of the pirates.

The leader explained that he had the protection of some senior Chinese naval officers and tankers being used to off-load our cargo were ships previously hijacked. Their crews were killed, he told me, and the ships, with false papers, were sold to a dummy Chinese company which was really a front for some rogue Chinese naval officers.

'Only your Chief Officer will be allowed outside the mess room during the transfer. He is Indonesian and can be passed off as one of us. He will operate the main cargo pumps in the control room. You will make his position clear to him.'

So the atmosphere was very tense on all sides. Mutual trust was evidently not a feature of this stage of the operation. To intimidate the crew and ensure their obedience, the pirates had begun to boast of previous exploits. In particular, they talked of a vessel they had hijacked which had carried an Indian crew of sixteen. The Captain of this ship, they alleged, had

had his wife and young son with him. The Thais among the pirates had boasted that the entire crew had been killed and the Captain's wife gang-raped prior to being killed. They told other similar tales and certain members of my crew were convinced of their authenticity. I was sceptical, but as a tactic to keep people under control it was certainly effective.

At 5.00 p.m. as I had been advised, our engines stopped and we were locked in the mess room. After twenty minutes or so we could hear that two vessels had come alongside. The Chief Officer was then taken to the cargo control room to operate the remote cargo pumps. The *Petro Ranger* was to discharge into the two tankers, but the tanks containing the automotive diesel oil were being pumped out first.

The Chief Officer later reported that he was required to change over the tanks which the pirates, despite the valves being marked, still did not understand how to do. He was dressed in their fashion, a balaclava was put on his head and a knife was held at his back as he changed over the valves. He was instructed to keep his eyes lowered at all times, but he managed to get a glimpse of the tankers' hulls, which were painted orange.

The eight hours during which we were locked in the mess room were unnerving and uncomfortable. We didn't know whether the next time the door was opened the pirates would enter and machine-gun the lot of us. The three stationary ships were tied together and were rolling in a light swell; also, it was rather unpleasant with only mineral water bottles to urinate into and no other toilet facilities.

The smaller tanker left first, at what time I'm not certain, and at 1.10 a.m. on the 23rd the cargo pumps fell silent and I assume that the larger tanker left then. Shortly afterwards our main engines restarted and we built up to full sea speed again. The mess room was

unlocked, use of the toilets and showering facilities
were restored and we were given a meal.

By this time we were considerably further north
than our legitimate voyage would have taken us and
the airconditioning made the mess room very cold.
I requested blankets and we were issued with them.
We settled down to sleep, still in great discomfort from
our tied wrists. My mental discomfort was as great as
the physical—only part of the cargo could have been
so far discharged. What was intended for the remain-
der? And what was intended for us?

The pirate leader, for some reason, seemed very
concerned to keep me abreast of what was happening.
He advised me later that morning that two of his men
had been sent ashore to collect a cash payment for the
cargo we had discharged. I had no idea of where we
were in Chinese waters or where the transfer had taken
place but I couldn't help making calculations. The
leader told me that it would take the tankers about
fourteen hours to deliver the stolen fuel. Assuming the
ships' speeds at about ten knots, that would make the
delivery point approximately 140 miles away.

Still filling me in thoroughly, Herman said that it
would take about 36 hours for the two pirates travel-
ling on board a 4000-tonne tanker to return with the
money. This tanker would unload the rest of the diesel
fuel. Apparently the syndicate no longer wanted the
jet fuel as they didn't have a buyer for it. Whether
this made our situation more or less perilous was
impossible for me to judge. As it was, we spent the
next 36 hours steaming back and forth in a restricted
area waiting for the third tanker to arrive.

It was back to the boring routine of being confined
in the mess room, tied at the wrists most of the time,
the crew eating meals in two shifts and me dining
alone. And that bloody movie, *Titanic*.

To this day I am puzzled by the pirates' behaviour
towards us as hostages. The classic technique is to keep

hostages disoriented by depriving them of a sense of night and day and by limiting toilet and bathing facilities, disturbing sleep and providing inadequate and inappropriate food. Nothing like this was done. As I have said, from time to time the pirates told frightening stories of their bloodier exploits (the equivalent of the propaganda terrorists spout in political hostage situations), but they didn't convince every member of the crew and the stories wore thin. As to why Herman saw fit to give me point by point details of the operation (other than his initial quiet boasting), I can only guess. Perhaps he was not as confident of the outcome as he might have been and was, in a way, sharing his uncertainty. He seemed almost to be asking my advice about his plans. I very carefully gave him nothing.

The cook finished his duties at 6.00 p.m. and should have been back with the rest of us soon after, but about twenty minutes later he was found to be missing. This threw the pirates, still unsure and edgy about the arrival of the third tanker, into a panic. An immediate count was organised in the mess room and we numbered twenty, one short. Leaving three guards, the rest began a search of the ship, getting more alarmed as they went. Apparently they feared he might have jumped overboard. I gathered from this that we must have been close to shore or other vessels.

They looked last where I would have looked first, in his cabin, and found him, a devout Muslim, with his prayer mat spread and wearing his cap, deep in prayer, totally unaware of the chaos he'd caused. He was returned quietly to us. He explained that in all the tension and confusion he'd neglected his prayers and was trying to make amends. The pirate leader summoned me for a brief meeting and it was arranged that all praying was to be done in the large cargo control room where the guards could keep those praying in sight. Neither Herman nor I were Muslims, but we both recognised the importance to those in the crew who were of praying several times a day.

At this point I should add that, in an effort to lighten the men's spirits, I encouraged them to refer to our place of captivity not as the mess room but as 'Club Med'.

Each day I had moved around among the men, spending a little time with all of them, reassuring them that things would turn out okay and that, one way or another, they would get home safely. As well as watching the pirates' mental states, I also kept a close eye on the crew as some of them were clearly more traumatised than I at first thought. The Third Officer, the Filipino fitter and three of the young sailors could stay awake for three nights in a row. I made sure all the men ate three meals a day but I couldn't order them to sleep, with the result that I could see them losing weight and becoming listless as time went by. 'Haunted' would be the best word to describe them. In hindsight, I can see how I became a part-time psychiatrist. I had to reassure the crew that all would be OK eventually, but without building up their hopes to the point the pirates became suspicious. The pirates were so nervy and agitated at this time that the slightest hint from the crew's behaviour that they weren't as demoralised as the pirates thought could have had disastrous consequences for all of us.

This was worrying because, apart from the suffering of the men themselves, it was difficult to judge how the pirates would react if a crew man really 'flipped out' as some of them seemed close to doing. The Bangladeshis reacted entirely differently, seeming to want to do nothing except eat and sleep. I noted that the Indonesians were the closest-knit group and handled things in their own way, showing little of their inner feelings.

So I had a lot on my mind: would the thugs' fear of the senior pirates eventually push them over to our side or was this wishful thinking? Would the pirates dispose of us by stages, getting rid of the less useful ones first? Of course I am human and spent many hours thinking of my wife and daughters, wondering how they were coping and who, if anyone, was looking for us.

My main mood, given my kind of temperament, was annoyance. The most difficult thing to do was to remain outwardly calm as displays of temper would do no one any good. The Indonesians were the best sources of information on the state of the pirates because they were of the same nationality as most of them and understood each other best. They appeared to handle the situation better than most of the others, but only so long as they stuck together as a group.

Monitoring all this, I didn't realise the strain I was under. I didn't have much appetite but hardly noticed that I was losing weight. I was aware that I wasn't sleeping much as I found the light being on for 24 hours a day disturbed my sleep pattern. Not being physically active you don't need much sleep perhaps, but poor sleeping takes a mental and emotional toll.

A peculiar thought occurred to me frequently at this time: *if I survive this, no one's actually going to believe it really happened*. The whole thing could be regarded as 'unreal' as, in a strange way, it seemed so to me— although rationally I knew it was all too real. Of course, I had no idea of what the outside world knew or didn't know.

I felt, for most of the time, neither fear nor bravado. My overriding thought most waking moments was: *how the hell do I get out of this?*

Day nine of the ordeal, 25 April, was a day of mood swings. The promised third tanker did not arrive within the expected time frame. Herman had apparently lost contact with his principals in China and he and his men became edgy and aggressive. Understandably so, as they may have thought they had been done out of their money.

The *Petro Ranger*'s radio officer was brought into the picture at this point (the pirates still not being sure how to operate the ship's communications systems), and contact was made with the two members of the gang who had been sent to collect payment for the first part of the cargo and were now aboard the third tanker. They assured their leader that all was well. They had the money and were on their way back with supplies of food and twelve cases of beer.

Although most of the pirates were ostensibly Muslims, it should not be imagined that they were different from others. I have seen Muslim seamen become enthusiastic drinkers in port when circumstances permitted. News of the money, the food and the beer restored the pirates' good spirits. The new arrangement was to meet up with the third tanker the next day. More boredom, more waiting.

8

The big mistake

The following day, 26 April, was the tenth day of our captivity. Again the pirates became sombre and the Radio Officer was called to the radio room to try and contact the third tanker, which was running late. He did this and a rendezvous was arranged for 2.00 p.m. There were changes to the plan, however. Instead of the expected 4000-tonne tanker, the one on its way was smaller, only 1000 tonnes, and they were advised that a fourth tanker would arrive on the 27th and take all the remaining cargo.

This is the point at which I believe it all started to go wrong for Herman and his gang.

At 10.00 a.m., foolishly, the pirates called the other tanker on the international calling channel 16 on the VHF and this signal was picked up by a Chinese patrol boat in the vicinity.

I became aware of some of this when I was being taken from my shower. Instead of being escorted down to the mess room I was told to wait in my cabin while three of the pirates changed their clothes and hid their weapons in my day room. They stood guard, ensuring that I stayed in the bedroom. After about fifteen minutes they ushered me out and instructed me to look aft out of one of the small windows. I saw a boat

I was told was a Marine Police boat departing.[8] Evidently the pirates were satisfied that they had coped with this intrusion as the Chinese had seemed satisfied with the false ship's documents.

At approximately two o'clock our aimless cruising stopped. A 1000-tonne tanker came alongside the *Petro Ranger* and the discharge of more diesel fuel began. Again we were locked in the mess room but it was impossible not to become aware of the jubilation outside. The two couriers had returned with suitcases full of US dollars, fresh food and the twelve cases of beer.

I later learned that the beer was not for the pirates, at least not all of it. We were to be given our share to lull us into a false sense of security. The syndicate had found a buyer for the jet fuel in China and the 4000-tonne tanker due the next day would complete the discharge of the diesel oil and return for the jet fuel. We would then become completely surplus to requirements and, with us made drunk or sleepy by the beer, I assume the plan was to machine-gun us and dispose of our bodies in the time-honoured fashion.

So, in the mid-afternoon the pirates felt optimistic and on top of the situation, but by 5.00 p.m. panic had set in as they could see that the patrol boat was returning. Some kind of an inspection of the vessel was anticipated because we were cleared out of the mess room and rushed down to the accommodation area on the lower deck where we were locked into the crew's cabins. The cabins were small and with four men locked inside each it was a tight squeeze.

At this point one of the few amusing incidents in the whole episode occurred. I was put in a cabin with the Radio Officer, the Chief Officer and one crew man. The Radio Officer was weeping.

'I was going to kill him,' he said repeatedly.

'What? What d'you mean?' I replied, thinking he meant a particular pirate.

He explained that when we'd all been in the mess

PETRO-PIRATES

FORM 22
IMMIGRATION ACT
(CHAPTER133)

Regulation 31(1)

IMMIGRATION REGULATIONS
CREW LIST

*Name/Identification No. of *Vessel/Train <u>MT Wilby</u>   'Master/Owner/Charterer <u>Sea King Shipping Co</u>

Agents in Singapore _____

Last place of embarkation <u>Singapore</u> _____ Date of arrival _____

Next destination <u>Hongkong</u> _____ Date of proposed departure _____

No	Name	Sex	Date of Birth	Nationality	Travel Document No	Expiry Date of Travel Document	Duties on Board
1	Herman	M	22/9/51	Indonesian	E.008328	22/9/2000	Master
2	Arsyad Ibrahim	M	22/9/48	Indonesian	G.743492	18/3/2003	Chief Officer
3	Darman Djuki	M	12/4/54	Indonesian	G.406461	6/11/2002	Chief Enginee:
4	Kardi Wijaya	M	1/1/59	Indonesian	F.204251	30/4/1998	2nd Engineer
5	Imam Basroni	M	05/03/76	Indonesian	G.093545	13/6/76	A B
6	Supriyo Manat	M	17/12/72	Indonesian	G.255952	29/7/2002	A B
7	Munif Abidin	M	22/3/75	Indonesian	G.207729	10/7/2002	A B
8	Ahmad Ali	M	12/31/60	Indonesian	F.792297	17/1/2002	Oiler
9	Budi Santoso	M	20/3/73	Indonesian	G.415313	2/10/2002	Oiler
10	Supermadi	M	29/7/74	Indonesian	G.274851	16/8/2002	Oiler
11	Jamal	M	10/9/65	Indonesian	G.317421	18/8/2003	Chief Cook.
12	Hasanudin Karim	M	31/12/66	Indonesian	G.274170	12/8/2002	2nd Cook

Twelf Crew including Master.

M.T. WILBY

MASTER

5. This crew list for the MT *Wilby* proves that the
    pirates had no intention of letting us live.

room the Chief Engineer had constantly been bumping into him when moving to the wash basin, disturbing his sleep and rest. The Radio Officer also had noticed that when biscuits were being issued the Chief Engineer always burrowed down for a particular kind. This had irritated him and he said he'd been collecting the poison out of cockroach traps and had intended to coat these kinds of biscuits with it and kill the engineer but his plan had been thwarted by our being moved from the mess room.

I found it funny, even in the dangerous circumstances we were in; I've never been sure whether he was serious or not. If he was, then it was indicative of the strain we were all under.

At this time the cargo line between the *Petro Ranger* and the tanker had been quickly disconnected, but not the mooring lines. Armed soldiers and two officers from the patrol boat boarded and both ships were placed under Marine Police control. The ships were disconnected and both proceeded under army orders to a destination which I later found out was the outer harbour of the port of Haikou on the island province of Hainan in southern China. We arrived there at eleven o'clock at night.

I was to learn that the reason the transfer of cargo and other transactions had taken place so close to land (a mere 100 miles) was that all parties believed that the deal was being carried out under the protection of the local senior naval commander, or as I later came to believe, the PSB commander. I would also learn something of the extent of fuel smuggling in Hainan. The Chinese intended the island to become a tourist attraction which, given its beaches, scenery and subtropical climate, was a possibility. Consequently there was no leaded petrol allowed; all vehicles, military and civilian, ran on diesel or unleaded petrol. But there were only minor shipments of these fuels from the mainland to the island—virtually the whole of the island's fuel supply came from blackmarket sources, connived at by the officials.

The pirates and their collaborators had blundered into their worst nightmare in the shape of a non-corrupt general of the People's Liberation Army (PLA) who had recently been appointed to put a stop to smuggling and piracy in southern China. Not only had this unchecked lawlessness, with many corrupt officials involved, become an international embarrassment, it was costing China too much money in lost excise on smuggled goods. Equally importantly, too much hard currency (US dollars) was leaving the country. I later learned that the general had a colleague, a senior Commissar, also non-corrupt. This man had been placed in charge of the Marine Police, a separate body altogether from the navy.

Of course, I didn't know these details at the time but neither did the pirates. They intended to play their hand out and evidently still thought that their contacts in China could deal with any problems that might arise. A comfort to them, at this stage, was the pirates' belief that they might be guilty of smuggling, not of piracy and hijacking. The pirates compelled my Chief Officer to act as officer of the watch on the passage to Haikou with the threat that his family would be killed if he didn't cooperate. He was selected because the Malaysian Second and Third Officers were unable to speak Indonesian and, anyway, were too cowed by events to be of much use. This coopting of the Chief Officer was to cause problems later when the authorities took him to be one of the gang. He must have played his part well and who could blame him?

When we reached the anchorage in Haikou the small tanker was moored alongside and armed guards put on both vessels. Again, although I didn't know what precisely was happening, I had a sense that the time for making a break was rapidly approaching.

In the early hours of the morning of the 27th,

Herman decided to make an amalgamated crew list comprising his gang and the members of my crew, minus myself. He could present the Chinese authorities with all the passports, making a ship's complement of 32 men. This might seem like a large crew for a ship the size of the *Petro Ranger*, but crew sizes vary from ship to ship and it might not arouse suspicion. It shows that the pirate leaders, although deprived of contact with their principals, were still hopeful of getting clear of the mess. I was to be kept locked in a cabin below decks. Ebenezer Gakpey ('Benny'), a cadet officer, was also kept in the engine room and the lower deck. A Ghanaian, he was very big and very black and the pirates feared that he might attract some unwanted attention.

The advantage of the amalgamated crew list device was that it enabled my crew to move about the ship with the pirates and act apparently normally. By this time the pirates had thrown their firearms overboard because, in China, the illegal possession of guns is a more serious crime than most, including smuggling. The crew didn't know this but, anyway, the threat offered them was the same as that given to the Chief Officer: their families would be killed. It was enough to keep them, or most of them, under control. The pirates still had their machetes and knives and they may have demonstrated this to the crew.

At 7.00 a.m. the Chinese authorities ordered both ships to be brought closer to shore—an encouraging development for me, perhaps, though not for the pirates. The Marine Police officers then took Herman, my Chief Officer (being mistaken for a suspect), and one of the Indonesians I feel sure was an executioner, ashore to their headquarters for questioning. Herman spoke some Mandarin along with his other languages and presumably had some idea of what was going on. Being questioned about smuggling was not necessarily the end of the world.

It was a trying time for the Chief Officer, however. He'd been taken aside by the two pirates and told in no uncertain terms that the threat to his family was very real. They instructed him to pretend that he spoke nothing but Indonesian and that, as the questioning would be in English and/or Chinese, Herman would interpret for him. This would give Herman considerable control over what was said.

Thinking they had nothing to fear from one man, the pirates had taken the improvised handcuffs off when I was locked in the cabin. The cook, under escort, brought me food which was limited by this time pretty much to bread and tea. I also had a carton of cigarettes. I smoked far too much during this very stressful period.

The three men were held ashore from 9.00 a.m. on the 27th to 11.00 p.m. on the 28th and there was no comfort for me in what Herman told me on his return. He still believed that his influential contacts in China would see him through and, apparently not fully grasping the situation, he believed that the Chinese authorities were simply holding out for a bigger bribe. Even then I had a feeling that he was misreading the situation. If the Marine Police had been corrupt they would have acted in a completely different way from the outset. But there was no way to be sure.

9

Bats out of hell

Thirteen days after the pirates' attack, on 29 April, I turned 53. I spent the day locked up.

At 10.00 a.m. the authorities sent for my radio operator and the deputy leader of the pirates, who was supposed to know how to operate the radio but didn't. The authorities wanted to know what radio frequencies they had used when sending messages to the tankers. Although I was confined to the cabin I could still communicate in a hurried fashion with members of the crew. The pirates only left one entrance open to the lower decks' cabins and we worked out a system of knocks on my door to indicate when the pirates were on the upper decks. In that event I could open my cabin door from the inside and talk. I told the radio operator to seize this chance to tell the Marine Police the true story and for a few hours I had hopes that this might resolve the matter. But when I next spoke to him at about three o'clock he told me that he'd been too frightened to do as I'd said, so that hope was dashed. Although I could open the door from the inside, the pirates, under the impression that I had no allies among the crew and that their threats were sufficient to keep me and the crew in line, thought this didn't matter.

Herman had been told by the Marine Police that he had to take ashore all the money he'd received from the sale of the cargo already discharged and that the balance of the cargo would be confiscated with its value constituting the fine imposed for smuggling. This arrangement was to be notarised by lawyers for both parties. How the pirates managed to get a lawyer to act for them under these circumstances I never discovered. On the completion of the discharge of the confiscated cargo, a port clearance would be granted and the ship allowed to leave.

It has to be understood that the original name of the ship had been painted out and the name *Wilby* substituted. This was at the bow and stern and on all life jackets and equipment. Any deck or cabin fittings that carried the name *Petro Ranger* had been removed. The pirates had authentic papers for a non-existent ship in that name so it was effectively disguised, although none of this would have stood up to a thorough examination. In fact, Herman had told me that their documents were purchased from the Philippines consulate of a small 'flag of convenience' state for about $6000, five weeks beforehand.

Our situation was now utterly desperate. If the ship cleared the port that was the end of us. I had to reach the Chinese guards while they were still on the ship and I began making plans. The crucial thing was to find others to depend on because it couldn't be done alone. I spoke to several of the crew about the need to do something but the Chief Officer advised me not to do this. Most of the men, he said, weren't reliable or had been too terrified by the pirates' threats to their families to take any action. But Benny Gakpey and a seaman named Saini Ugie understood what was going on and volunteered to help me. Benny was well-educated, spoke perfect English and at 188 centimetres and with a powerful build and a serious character, he was a useful ally. Saini, from Sarawak, also well-educated with good English, was 173 centimetres, 24 years of age and resourceful. In character he was something of a larrikin, but he had the great advantage of being able to speak some Mandarin.

At this point it's worth noting that a good many of the crew aboard the *Petro Ranger*, although they held jobs as ordinary seamen and the like, were well-educated men. It's a fact that in the Third World a relatively low-level seaman can earn more than a skilled worker in an office job, and a ship's crew can contain men with the most unlikely talents and abilities.

Benny and Saini apparently had faith in my ability to judge the situation and make the right decisions. With crews from those parts of the world, the Captain of a ship becomes something like the head of the village. Provided he remains competent, calm and in control, his orders will be followed even in difficult situations. The first part of the plan I came up with was for Saini to visit the small tanker tied up alongside at the same time as the commanding officer of the soldiers positioned there went for his evening meal. He was to propose a meeting with the Chinese officer in charge on the 'monkey island', the uppermost deck on the *Petro Ranger* with a clear 360-degree view, by claiming to have information about the smuggling. He made contact and was able to arrange a later meeting, which suggests that at least some of the senior Marine Police suspected that there was more to the matter than met the eye. The time of the rendezvous was to be 12.30 a.m. on the 30th.

The next part of the plan was this: after the pirates had completed their rounds and were satisfied that I was where I should be and that the accommodation area was quiet they would move to the upper decks. Saini would signal from the stairwell that all was clear. Benny would then give three knocks and we would run up the internal stairs to the storm door on the engineer's deck. Like the other external doors to the accommodation, the storm door was not watched closely as it gave access only to the stairs leading to the bridge and monkey island. This area was off limits to all but the police guards.

I equipped myself with the only weapon to hand, a pair of desk scissors. I clasped them so I could use them to jab or slash if I encountered opposition and I was fully prepared to do so. At this point there was no room for hesitation, doubt or half-measures. Anyone who got in my way would suffer injury and I was ready to trample them to get to where I needed to be.

When we got the signal Saini and I, barefooted, took off like bats out of hell and dashed up the stairs, through the storm door and on up to the monkey island. All was quiet except for background marine machinery noises. As I recall, I spoke only one word at this time: 'Quick!' Benny, meantime, locked the door to my cabin from the inside so that any pirate checking from outside would think I was still locked in.

There were two soldiers on watch on the monkey island, an area about fifteen metres square, which was dark except for reflected light from the deck flood-lights. I must have looked a strange figure in my uniform shirt with epaulettes but barefooted and slightly out of breath. I hadn't showered for three days and had a three-day growth of beard. I handed my passport and the Malaysian government document identifying me as the master of the *Petro Ranger* to the army lieutenant while Saini did his best to explain things in Mandarin.[9]

The soldiers were surprised and excited but, in hindsight, I believe that they were waiting for something of this kind to happen. They must have been sceptical about Herman's account of the ship's activities. It was only much later, after I arrived home, that I realised that the extensive press coverage of the disappearance of the *Petro Ranger* would have excited Chinese suspicions as to the true identity of the *Wilby*.

They grasped the situation quickly. Saini returned to my cabin, where he put a rolled up blanket in the bunk to look like a sleeping figure and turned out all the lights so that everything would look as the pirates would expect it to. He and Benny then returned to their cabins.

A radio message was sent to army headquarters and a powerboat came out to collect my documents. I had to hope and pray that the Marine Police or, as I thought at that time, the PLA members I was dealing with were honest and not in league with the criminal elements that existed in the navy and the PSB. At 3.00 a.m. it looked as if I had backed the right horse. A large patrol boat arrived and anchored nearby. I was given an army jacket and cap and requested to stay on the monkey island so that if any pirate saw me in silhouette he'd think I was a soldier. It was a mild, clear night as I stood there, disguised as a member of the Chinese People's Liberation Army, something I could never in a million years have imagined happening to me. The port was visible, a picturesque sight, only three kilometres away.

One of the soldiers spoke a little English and told me that there were 30 armed soldiers on the patrol boat but that the commander wanted to wait until daylight before arresting the pirates as he thought that would give a better chance of doing it without casualties. And so it proved. At 7.00 a.m. the patrol boat drew up alongside the ship and the senior officer advised that those who had already been ashore for interviews had to return for a medical and to sign the statement they had discussed before. With them aboard the patrol boat the officer then said that the real crew of the ship should also board the patrol boat. They did so. Somehow word had passed around between them that I had escaped during the night and swum to the patrol boat. With their smokescreen of the amalgamated crew lifted and facing 30 heavily armed soldiers, the rest of the pirates gave themselves up without a fight.

Once everyone was on board the patrol boat I was required to take off my disguise and go down to identify the twelve pirates and nominate one of the ship's engineers to return on board to look after the generators and other machinery while the rest of the crew went ashore and things were sorted out. I appointed the Second Engineer.

And so, in a very orderly, military fashion, the hijacking of MT *Petro Ranger* came to an end. I felt immense relief, not realising that the second act of the drama was about to begin.

As a boy in Scotland, I was interested in only two alternative career paths: to play football for my beloved Glasgow Rangers or go to sea as a Navigating Officer. It became clear that I didn't have the talent to become a professional footballer, so on 18 May 1961, I set out on my first voyage as a Cadet Officer full of confidence and excitement, but never dreaming that I would have the unique experience of surviving a hijacking by pirates 37 years later.

Like anyone else at the age of sixteen, I thought of pirates in terms of Long John Silver and 'Yo, ho, ho and a bottle of Pimms'. By 1998 it was clear that piracy was very much a modern crime and, like all Captains, I read and digested the data on the subject collected by all the international maritime authorities. But when you're driving a car, you think other people have crashes, not you. Similarly, I thought a pirate attack might happen to someone else, but not to me. As well, no data had ever been issued regarding hijacking and I thought of piracy as the quick seizure of money and valuables and that's all. When I was told 'I only want the cargo', that raised other questions about *these* pirates' intentions and procedures.

When, much later, I was asked, 'What were you thinking about when you were tied up in the mess room for so long? Did you recall happy moments, such as the birth of your children, and other signposts along the road of life?' I've had to steel myself to answer politely, as the question bespeaks a quiet and sheltered life. When you are the master of a hijacked ship and become a hostage or prisoner, you are immediately confronted with a situation for which you have had no training. I suddenly had twenty traumatised shipmates and twelve pirates of uncertain temperament to contend with. As I've said, my chief thought was how to escape. I formed many plans in my mind but had to discard most of them as I could see that most had little chance of success. Also I wanted to avoid bloodshed if possible.

Before I went to sleep each night, however, my wife and daughters were always on my mind. I later learned that *their* worst fear was that I had lost my temper and had provoked the pirates into killing or beating me. Apart from my family, my focus was on escape and survival and I suggest that this focus is necessary to a successful outcome to a situation like the one I was in. Self-pity, regrets, reminiscences—all that could cause you to lose that focus and make you unprepared for the moment when, come what may, you have to act—cannot be allowed.

PART II

In Chinese waters

10

Out of the frying pan

When the patrol boat carrying my crew and the pirates
left for the Marine Police headquarters on Hainan,
the senior Marine Police officer, a colonel whose name
I never learned, his officers and staff immediately
began to question me. The Chinese all spoke at once,
one over the top of the other in loud, high-pitched
voices. The young woman officer acting as translator
had difficulty in keeping up with them and making
clear what they were asking. It became ludicrous; I
demanded a cup of coffee and walked out of the
meeting. If that's what being 'a fiery Scotsman' means,
then I suppose I am.

It became obvious that this method of obtaining
information wasn't going to work and an altogether
better way was found. I was asked to escort the colonel
and his staff around the ship's accommodation areas,
explaining where we had been kept at first and where
I had been confined towards the end. I hadn't seen
much of these areas in the past four days and I was
appalled at the filthy condition of the cabins and other
spaces.

Through this tour, which lasted approximately two
hours, one of the officers recorded all that was said and
done with a video camera. At about half past ten the

colonel politely suggested that I have a shave and a shower (I'd gone without either for four days and must have looked very scruffy) and get a few hours' sleep. He asked me if I was satisfied with the Marine Police's response to my request for help. Indeed I was, to this point at least, and I sincerely thanked him and all concerned on behalf of myself and my crew. This episode ended with video shots of the colonel and myself shaking hands and smiling in a friendly fashion.

After shaving and showering I lay down on the settee in my day room and immediately fell asleep. I woke up at about three o'clock, got dressed in my khaki uniform shirt, khaki trousers, shoes and socks and an hour later I was taken by a high-powered launch to be interviewed at headquarters. These Chinese launches are powered by five 250 horsepower engines and travel at between 50 and 60 knots—quite an experience.

On arrival at headquarters I was taken to a small conference room, given a Chinese meal and tea and left in comfort until 7.00 p.m. when an officer who spoke perfect English began the interview. The main topics covered were my personal details and information on the ship: the name of the owners in Singapore, the company's telephone number, where we had loaded in Singapore and the owners of the cargo in Saigon. Then I was asked to go back to the moment of the hijacking and estimate the position of the ship and the time of the attack.

'This interview will have to be suspended, Captain,' the officer said at about ten o'clock. 'And I regret to tell you that you and your crew will have to be kept in the jail in this building. This is the only place we can guarantee your safety until those involved in this matter have been caught.'

I could see the sense in this after what Herman had told me about the influence the syndicate could exert in this part of the world. In any case we were given no choice. The cell was large and very cold with bars on the windows, a barred door and a cement floor.[10] I asked about bedding and was brought a thin pile of last week's Chinese newspapers. And so I spent my first night of what I thought would be freedom locked in a Chinese jail. To keep the men's spirits up I recommended that they refer to the jail as the 'Haikou Hilton'.

At 7.00 a.m. the guards gave me a breakfast of dry bread and bottled mineral water. When I needed to use the toilet I was escorted by a guard. Things hadn't changed nearly as much from the time on the ship as I'd hoped. At 10.00 a.m. I was taken back upstairs to the conference area to resume being interviewed. But now I was told it would be a joint investigation—the Marine Police would be joined by officers of the PSB of the province of Hainan Island. In other words, the State Police.

During any joint session with the PSB in a large conference room with everyone seated around a big table, the Marine Police always made a video recording of the proceedings and I shortly came to understand why. The PSB were insisting that the ship was the *Wilby*, not the *Petro Ranger*. I quickly concluded that the PSB were acting in the interest of the pirates and realised as time went by that some of them at least were in league with the Chinese arm of the pirates' syndicate.

There were four PSB officers present and I remarked to the most senior of them that Chinese police must be paid a great deal more than their counterparts in Australia.

'What do you mean, Captain?'

I said, 'That Swiss Oris watch you're wearing would cost about $US5000 and that designer Dunhill handbag you use, I don't know how much that would cost. Even a corrupt Queensland policeman couldn't afford that stuff.'

This was the only time I ever saw any of the Chinese officials I dealt with sweat. This exchange was videoed and it was clear from the attitude of the PSB officer that he was not at all comfortable with being videoed during these proceedings. At noon there was a break for lunch. We resumed at about two o'clock and the senior PSB officer advised me that he believed the ship was the MT *Wilby*. This was tantamount to calling me a liar and I became angry and hotly denied it.

Then an extraordinary event took place. A man who I took to be a Marine Police officer, although he was nondescriptly dressed in a T-shirt, dialled a number on his mobile phone and walked around the conference table towards the senior PSB man. But, instead of handing the phone to him, he at first held it to my ear so that I could hear the speaker, who was using both Chinese and English. Then he quickly gave the phone to the PSB officer. The person on the other end of the phone, whose voice I had recognised, was Captain Chan, Operations Manager for Petroships in Singapore. He verified that the ship was indeed the *Petro Ranger* and said that all crew details were being faxed to the police headquarters as he spoke. The man with the mobile phone, I learned a good deal later, was the Commissar who'd been appointed to clean up smuggling and corruption in the southern provinces.

The Commissar then indicated that I should leave the room with him. We went to an office where an interpreter from the Marine Police spoke in English on the phone to Petroships verifying that all members of the crew of the ship were safe and well. From there the Commissar, accompanied by an interpreter, took me downstairs to the cell where the crew were being held and asked me to reassure them that things were being sorted out. The news had been sent to Singapore that we were all safe and this would be relayed to their families. And they would be released very soon.

Then it was back up to the offices where I was told I'd be returned to the ship at 6.00 p.m.

'What about the crew?' I asked.

'They will have to stay here for a time because they would impede the search we are going to make of the ship. We are looking for money and weapons. They will have to remain ashore until this has been completed.'

Which was a polite way of saying they would stay in jail. I had previously told the Marine Police that they'd be held responsible for any further damage to the ship as the only officer left aboard, the Second Engineer, could hardly keep an eye on all the machinery for 24 hours a day. I was allowed to take a further two officers with me and I selected the Chief Officer and the Third Engineer as they'd shown themselves to be the most responsible of my officers.

I found the behaviour of the Chinese officials very peculiar. It was easy enough to distinguish between the Marine Police in their green uniforms and the PSB in khaki, but the officers had the habit of changing their epaulettes (which indicated their rank) so you could never be sure who was who or what rank he held.

The conference room was well appointed with very comfortable office chairs and everyone was supplied with iced coconut water, a popular drink in Hainan, which is famous for its coconuts. It's worth noting that the western strictures against smoking haven't reached China. Everyone seemed to smoke in the meetings and, as there were no ashtrays, you simply dropped the butt on the tile floor and stepped on it. Offering, accepting and exchanging cigarettes was a normal part of social behaviour. Security was very tight in this building. The cells were on the ground floor and the offices and conference rooms on various levels above. When an interrogation was going on the power to the lifts was cut. There was no lighting in the stairwells but as soon as anyone entered a stairwell to go down, a laser beam switched on a light and a bang sounded indicating where the person was.

When the Chief Officer and the Second Engineer were released we started up the stairs to the Commissar's office, which was on the fifth floor. At this moment, for the first and only time in my life, I truly thought I'd been shot. The laser beam that activated the lights also set off this warning bang which sounded for all the world like a gunshot. Contrary to popular belief, you do not get a weak feeling in the bowels or anywhere else. You freeze and feel as if you've lost ten years of your life. The Chinese thought it was amusing. I told them in the Australian vernacular what I thought. Perhaps it's just as well they didn't understand as it could have sent us back to jail.

I had to agree not to impede the soldiers in their search or touch or remove anything that might have belonged to the pirates. The Chinese officers couldn't stop laughing when I told them that the pirates were now wearing our clothes as they preferred them on account of their quality. This was the first really light moment in the episode. Up until then I had begun to doubt that Chinese officials had a sense of humour.

After this meeting, one of the officers asked me if I'd like to see the pirate leader and I said I would. I was shown to a room where Herman was sitting, looking pretty confident and, to my considerable anger, wearing some of my clothes and my newest pair of black shoes, bought just prior to leaving Singapore.

He smiled cynically and said, before I could say a word, 'No worries, Captain. A couple of hundred thousand dollars in the right place and I'll be out of here.'

This was the man who had threatened the lives of my wife and daughters and would not have hesitated to kill the crew and myself. I strongly suspect that he'd killed in his other ventures. Knowing this, frustrated at being held hostage and under considerable stress after ensuring the safety of the crew and contriving to escape, I saw red. I grabbed a machine pistol from one of the guards, fully intending to shoot the grinning pirate. Of course, I was restrained.

As I was leaving the headquarters building I passed a room holding the six young pirates all seated at a table, under guard, and all scribbling away. To my surprise, Saini was there as well, standing by the door.

Curiosity got the better of me and I stopped. 'What are you doing here?' I asked him.

He said that these six were writing out their 'confessions' and the Marine Police were using him as interpreter and translator because he could handle both Indonesian and Malaysian and translate the statements into English. So Saini's linguistic abilities had at least got him out of the cell for a while.

The officer who accompanied us down to the power-boat which was to take us out to the ship was the same English speaker who had initially interviewed me. I asked him when they had discovered that I was telling the truth about the ship and the crew.

'At 10.00 a.m. this morning, Captain,' he replied.

'Why didn't you tell me then?'

His look was full of surprise. 'Captain, you never let the people you are interrogating know what information you already have.'

It became clear to me then that in reality it was the PSB officers who had been interrogated without them being aware of it. The Chinese must have known what was up from monitoring western news broadcasts. But their investigation methods are all their own. They consider that they have plenty of time, and in this case they played a waiting game, letting the pirates and possibly the PSB dig deep holes for themselves.

On board the Second Engineer told me that during my time ashore a large group of soldiers had been on board searching for the money the pirates had received for the contraband cargo they'd sold. I believe they recovered approximately $US320 000. They also found

three or four of the large machetes, several of the
balaclava masks and the improvised 'O' ring handcuffs.

The Second Engineer, an Indonesian, burst into
tears and exclaimed that if he'd only known the money
had been hidden in his cabin he'd have taken it and
hidden it in the engine room where it couldn't be
found. He said that with that amount of money he
could have bought half of Jakarta, referring to the deep
economic crisis Indonesia was in at the time. We
managed to console him and found a funny side to the
events of the past 48 hours.

I looked around for towels and bed linen and found
a package of forged documents left behind by the
pirates. But the main find (in the Radio Officer's cabin)
was a collection of false ship's documents and bills of
lading for another vessel which was next in line to be
hijacked after us. After its valuable cargo of palm oil
had been disposed of, the ship was intended to be
disguised and sold under the name MT *Surin*. These
were legal documents issued by the same office in
Manila as the ones for the MT *Wilby*. The ship's name
and particulars were false, but the documents themselves were perfectly official and legal (see Appendix B).

I didn't feel honour bound to keep my undertaking
not to interfere with anything belonging to the pirates.
This was hard evidence of the organisational structure
of the pirate syndicate and I wanted to make sure it
fell into the right hands. I took the documents.

That night was the first I spent in comparative
comfort since the attack. The next day the police
continued their search for weapons, money and any
other evidence they could find. They were thorough
and kept a video record of everything they did and
found. Every day the Marine Police sent out food,
water and cigarettes for their men and I never saw
them take any item, food or anything else, from the
ship.

11

Denise flies out

At 6.45 p.m. on 1 May, Captain Liew phoned Denise with the news that the ship had been located and that the crew and I were safe. She immediately phoned DFAT in Canberra with the news and gave them the fax and telephone number of the Marine Police headquarters which Petroships had given her. DFAT checked and phoned back at 9.00 p.m. confirming the information. Between 7.00 p.m. and 9.00 p.m. Denise called various family members and close friends and gave them the good news. Linda and Denise then sent me a fax care of the Marine Police headquarters in Haikou. They let me know that they knew I was in the land of the living and welcomed me 'back from the dead'.[11]

The initial press reports were cautiously optimistic, although inaccurate about the number of crew members and certain details of the ship's movements. Petroships was sticking to the story that a telex had been received from the vessel on 17 April and that they were the 'operators' of the *Petro Ranger* rather than the owners. The media were driving Denise and Linda crazy, besieging the house and lining the street. They could not understand why Denise still wouldn't talk to them. Her reasons were simple: as far as details were concerned, they knew as much as she did.

Denise's greatest surprise came when I telephoned at 11.00 a.m. for two minutes only on 2 May. Denise went to church on the following Sunday and prayers were offered in thanks for my survival. That day she sent another fax which I still have as a treasured possession. It reads:

Dear Ken

How wonderful to get your phone call yesterday and to know you are okay. Thought we'd let you know you are headline news here.

The media is trying to contact you direct for a big media conference or comment. Please don't talk to them until we're together as a family and only if you want to.

We're all well and anxiously looking forward to your homecoming or until I see you in Singapore, Hong Kong or wherever.

Lots of love,

Denny.

Denise was waiting for the Australian Consul to arrive at Haikou on Sunday so that a time for us to meet could be arranged. She was told by DFAT that the plane was cancelled on Saturday due to bad weather but it was hoped it would be rescheduled for the next day.[12] DFAT advised her at 6.00 p.m. that the consular officials had arrived in Haikou but rough seas prevented launches getting to the ship. After we spoke on the phone again the next day she decided to fly to Hong Kong and wait there until she got permission to enter China. She was prepared to wait for as long as it took.

DFAT arranged for her to be met in Hong Kong and installed in a hotel. She spent a good deal of her time in the Consulate waiting for news. She eventually got the all clear to fly to China, but not until 15 May. On 16 May at 8.40 a.m. she flew to Haikou by Dragonair and was met by a consular official and escorted to the hotel. We were reunited at Marine Police headquarters at 11.30 a.m., almost a month after the drama had begun. But there were still many obstacles to clear before we could enjoy that happy event.

12

'Captain, this money must be returned'

At about ten o'clock in the morning of 2 May, a launch came out and an interpreter came to my quarters and handed me a mobile phone. I was able to call home for the first time since leaving Singapore. The ever-present video camera was running through this first phone call home but I ignored it. It was a phone call I'll never forget. My only regret was that I could only speak to my wife and younger daughter. Wendy was stationed at the RAAF base Edinburgh in South Australia and I was only allowed one call. I felt immense relief and happiness in making contact and on a practical level it indicated that the Chinese were now prepared to allow information about me and the ship to reach the outside world. This increased my feelings of security. I already felt that I was dealing with an honest element among Chinese officialdom, but the knowledge that the western world and press now knew of our existence was an added guarantee of our safety.

At the conclusion of my phone call video shots were taken of handshakes all round and the Chinese officials departed for headquarters, leaving only the permanent guards aboard both ships. I was left to my own devices. I would have liked to have tuned in to news from outside China, but the pirates had dismantled the communications systems and the police removed my TV set—the only thing they took. So, although safe and able to set my loved ones' minds at rest, I still had only a qualified freedom. The rest of the day passed quietly, giving me plenty of time to mull over my situation.

Sunday in Haikou was quiet and I spent most of the day assessing the damage to the accommodation, the radio room and the engine room. The Second and Third Engineers assured me that once the crew was back on the ship the main engine and auxiliaries only needed an update on routine maintenance which had been neglected during the time of the pirates' presence. It wasn't going to take long to get things back in order.

Damage to the accommodation was limited to various items of smashed furniture and the removal of things that had identified the ship as the *Petro Ranger*. But this could be easily repaired back in Singapore. However, the radio room and its equipment had been badly damaged and contrary to Chinese media reports which were picked up and distorted by the western media, no Chinese technicians were detailed to make repairs to the equipment.[13] No repairs were carried out.

The Chinese did not want us to have free access to the outside world and the media. I was never allowed on the navigation bridge as this was where the soldiers guarding the ship had their command post. This was absolutely off limits and it was the only place at that time where there were any functioning communications devices—mainly VHF sets.[14]

At 4.00 p.m. that afternoon, a launch came out and I was told to go ashore and meet with Mr Tan, executive director of Petroships, who was accompanied by Captain Jerries from Petroships' office and a Mr Choong from the regional office of the International Maritime Bureau (IMB), based in Kuala Lumpur. This meeting, which was to prove that I was alive and well, lasted barely two or three minutes. The Chinese ended it quickly, permitting no further conversation. When Mr Tan protested loudly at this two soldiers threw him out of the building, literally threw him down the front steps of the headquarters building. Captain Jerries and Mr Choong had more sense; they kept their mouths shut and left quietly.

I had time only for a brief exchange with Captain Jerries in which I signalled that I wanted to relieve myself of command of the *Petro Ranger*, citing health reasons and the effects of the long period of stress. I requested that the company should find a replacement. This was a deliberate strategy on my part. It appeared that the Chinese were entertaining grave suspicions surrounding the activities of Petroships and it seemed wise to place some distance between the company and myself. Other than this brief meeting to confirm my existence, the Chinese would have no communication with Petroships' people in China, nor would they deal with Mr Choong from the IMB.

After this brief meeting I was taken out to the parade ground in front of the headquarters building—a large cement square with pillboxes at the gates for the sentries and the Chinese flag flying above it—where the crew, who had been brought from the jail, were assembled. The Commissar said that when the Marine Police had seized the ship the pirates had given each member of the crew a $US100 bill as compensation for personal effects that had been used or damaged and for the money that had been taken from them after the attack.

'Captain,' he said, 'this money must be returned.'

I was dumbfounded because I knew nothing about this. No member of the crew had mentioned it to me. I said, 'No, we haven't got any American money. I've got some Australian money and any the crew might have would be Malaysian, or Indonesian or Singaporean.'

But the Commissar insisted and requested me to order the men to return any American money. Still sceptical about this accusation, I informed the crew of what the Commissar had told me and asked if there was any truth in it. Suddenly $100 bills appeared and the soldiers collected $US2000, although the Fourth Engineer tried to hang on to his $100. As these bills were part of the money that had been paid for the stolen fuel they were evidence, and such was the thoroughness of the Marine Police that they couldn't let it pass. When the money was collected, the Commissar and I counted it, confirmed the amount and I signed a document to that effect.

What this showed was that the Chinese must have been interrogating the pirates down to the last detail and that they now knew everything that had happened and were crossing every 't' and dotting every 'i'.

I believe that it was at this time that the Chinese officers told me that Petroships was suspected of being part of the pirate conspiracy; and this was why I wasn't permitted to have any contact with them and no company representatives were allowed near the ship. At the time I found this hard to believe, but a seed of doubt had been planted in my mind.

As far as I'm aware, the crew never voluntarily offered any assistance to the pirates; everything they did was under threat of harm to them or their families. So I believe that the handing over of money to the crew by the pirates was an attempt to ingratiate themselves—to show that they, rather than the Chinese Marine Police, were the good guys. But I have to admit that I exhibited real anger towards the officers and crew, I think for the first and only time, on the launch back to the ship. I had been prepared to advise the Commissar firmly that the men would never have accepted money from the pirates whereas they had. In my rage, I questioned the parenthood of all of them along with other insults.

In my opinion the crew, or many of them, were as fearful of the Chinese as they were of the pirates.

In the first two weeks in Haikou, even though the pirates were being held in the Marine Police jail, the crew still entertained doubts that they would be set free. The Han Chinese tend to treat all nationalities in the surrounding area with a disregard amounting to something like contempt. Their attitude to my crew reflected this; although they were never treated unkindly, their treatment was very cold and impersonal and the seamen remained apprehensive about Chinese officialdom.

Once these money matters had been sorted out on the parade ground all members of the crew were returned to the ship. After three nights and four days in jail, under the severe conditions I've described, this was a very great relief to them.

And so another phase of the drama ended. Captain and crew of the MT *Petro Ranger* were back on board their ship—not under circumstances that any of us could have imagined, but at least unharmed and safe from the threat of machetes and machine-guns. But the legal, diplomatic and other wheels that would eventually lead to our freedom were to turn very slowly.

On Monday 4 May, I let the crew rest. Many of them were still walking around in a semi-traumatised state and I thought it best to leave them to sort themselves out. At 9.30 a.m. a launch came out and I was taken to Marine Police headquarters where, to my great surprise, I met Graham Pearce, the Australian Vice-Consul from the Guangzhou Consulate. Graham, a tallish, fortyish, fair-haired bloke, was accompanied by his wife, Daisy, who was originally from Hong Kong and of course spoke Mandarin. Also in the party were a Mr Li from the Chinese Foreign Affairs Office and another Chinese official who seemed to be a go-between—liaising between the Marine Police and the Chinese Foreign Office.

My meeting with Graham Pearce and his wife lasted for about two hours and the Chinese gave us total freedom to talk. This was the first opportunity I'd had to give an account to an outsider of what had happened from the time of the attack to the present. I gave Graham as detailed an outline as I could. Also, a great boon, I was allowed to use Graham's mobile phone to call Denise and have a private, extended conversation with her. She said she was flying to Hong Kong and was hoping to join me as soon as possible. That lifted my spirits considerably although, from my experience of Chinese bureaucracy so far, I doubted that it would be as easy as that. I was also allowed to phone the Australian Consul General in Guangzhou, Ms Zena Armstrong, and tell her that I was well and was receiving every possible assistance from Graham and Daisy.

Nevertheless, although guilty of no crime, I was still effectively a captive. Negotiations were opened with the Chinese as to why I was being detained in China and the official answer was that I was 'assisting with their investigations'. Graham offered to give me a mobile phone but the Chinese wouldn't permit that. Contrary to all media reports, the Australian consular officer was not allowed to see me on a daily basis. I was only allowed to meet with him every three or four days.

I was offered the opportunity to go to the markets but I refused, knowing that this was just a propaganda game. I would simply have been driven to the markets and back again, allowing the Chinese to claim that I'd been free to go shopping.

None of this was ever reported accurately. In fact, Graham Pearce was the only source of information Petroships had. None of the Chinese officials would speak with the company people. The press release issued soon after this by the IMB and widely publicised was based on information released by the Australian

Consulate, the only outside body the Chinese were prepared to deal with at this time.

On my return home I discovered, through various people, that although the IMB publicised itself in the fashion it did, in reality it is simply a data gathering organisation funded by voluntary contributions from ship owners and their various shipping associations and really carries very little authority. In fact, the Piracy Reporting Centre (PRC) in Kuala Lumpur has been described as being as effective as 'holding an Alcoholics Anonymous meeting in a brewery'! The IMB carries limited credibility, therefore, and its staff are recruited only from the Indian sub-continent and Malaysia. It would be better served by a staff comprised of the following nations—Japan, Taiwan, Hong Kong, China and Europe—for the simple reason the majority of ships in the China Sea are owned by these nations who, in turn, are more aware of the problem of hijacking/piracy and smuggling. This is a view shared by many senior members of the international shipping community, but due to their positions they cannot express it as I am now free to do.

In fact, the IMB only gained recognition after my actions during and after the hijacking of the *Petro Ranger* and can take no credit for the subsequent reforms enacted in China and Indonesia. Quite frankly, it was I, through my escape to the Chinese, who brought hijacking at sea to the world's attention, thus inspiring the positive actions taken to eliminate this cruel practice.

At this point the whole affair was being complicated by various layers of suspicion. One thing was very clear: the PSB was completely excluded from all dealings with consuls or foreign representatives at this stage. The PSB was not allowed aboard the ship. In short, other than the meeting on 1 May in which they participated with such discomfort, they were kept out of the loop.

At around 1.00 p.m., Graham Pearce and Daisy were politely told that they had to leave and I was returned to the ship. The Chinese media told the western press that I was permitted to go on shopping expeditions and move around freely. It was quite untrue. It never happened.

We then had a break from official visits and, after reviewing the mental condition of the crew, I decided that it would be better for them to be occupied. I got the Chief Officer and Chief Engineer up to my quarters and gave orders that normal duties would be resumed. I particularly wanted the accommodation cleaned, scrubbed and disinfected and routine maintenance carried out. There were meals to be prepared and laundry to be done. I advised the Chinese guards on the bridge of this as there were still areas of the ship that were off limits to us. Saini, the seaman who'd been of such great assistance in the escape, acted as interpreter and did a good job. He wanted no particular recognition for the courageous part he'd played.

With the TV set taken away and no radios I amused myself at night by playing music tapes (not Indian music) and reading, but the time hung heavy.

On Wednesday 6 May, along with the seven Malaysian crew members, I was taken ashore. I was to meet Graham Pearce and Daisy and the Malaysian crew were to meet their consul, who had now arrived in Haikou. But the Chinese treated me very differently from the Malaysians. I was allowed two hours with my people and Mr Li of the Chinese Foreign Office. I was allowed to phone my wife, who had now flown to Hong Kong, and also my younger daughter. We also tried to contact my older daughter at RAAF Edinburgh but she was out of her office and I had to leave a message on her answering machine.

By contrast, Mr Li took the Malaysian Consul to meet his nationals and the Chinese allowed him only twenty minutes. He was able to check that their passports were genuine and that was about all. It was quite unfair, but the Chinese didn't even pretend to be fair in such matters. The Malaysian officer who'd disgraced himself before and during the attack had earlier complained to me that he hadn't been able to see his consul for as long as I had. I wasn't sympathetic and just said, 'Tell it to the Chinese.' He saw the consul now and was still complaining about this and that. The other crew members more or less sent him to Coventry, which he thoroughly deserved.

By this time I was agitating to be allowed to leave China or at least to be able to stay in a hotel when my wife arrived. Graham Pearce put it to Mr Li that, under the Chinese criminal code, I should either be charged with some offence or be allowed to leave. Mr Li undertook to make enquiries along those lines but, having seen how slowly things moved in China, I wasn't hopeful.

The Marine Police launches' dock was only a short walk from the headquarters and, as we made our way there, I was surprised to find that a group of PSB officers along with a couple of armed guards were going out to the ship with us. More surprisingly, Herman, the pirate leader, was going as well. This was the only time I felt any sympathy for him. He was now bare-footed and could only shuffle along with difficulty and was being encouraged to walk faster by vicious jabs with rifle butts. He was in agony and I could feel those rifle butts as if they were hitting me.[15] He wasn't the confident figure he'd been a while back and it was evident that he'd taken a severe beating. I didn't speak to him and in fact he was under orders to remain silent and to keep his head down.

The presence of the pirate leader created some alarm among my Malaysian crew members but I re-assured them that everything was under control. I had no idea why he was being taken to the ship but he was clearly no threat. On getting back to the *Petro*

Ranger the three armed Marine Police plus an inter-preter came to my quarters and requested I sign a document giving my permission for the PSB to inspect the ship and search for evidence of piracy. I refused because the document was in Chinese, but I agreed to give verbal permission for the PSB to do as they wished as long as it was under Marine Police supervision. That's the way it was done: the PSB men being closely attended by armed Marine Police and an interpreter with, once again, everything being videoed.

This caused a lot of ill feeling between the two investigating authorities with me caught in the middle. By this time I was so fed up with the double-dealing and lying going on that I couldn't have cared less and I became somewhat difficult to deal with. When a Chinese raised his voice I simply raised mine louder.

Why the pirate leader was brought to the ship and what the PSB had him do there I never found out. It remains one of the mysteries of the whole event and, in fact, I never saw Herman again. Of course, I hoped to see him in court and to give evidence against him but that never happened. Why that didn't happen is another part of the story.

The next day fresh stores of food arrived with Mr Tan aboard the Petroships agent's launch. As before, Mr Tan wasn't allowed to speak to me but he gave an envelope to the agent, who passed it up to me. The envelope contained $US2000 to enable me to pay for things the ship might need, like fresh water. Now I was reluctant to accept it after all the fuss there'd been about the *other* $2000. I thought, *God, anyone in China with 2000 American dollars is bound to be suspected of something*. I said I wouldn't take it but the Chinese who could speak English burst out laughing.

'You take it, Mister Captain. We've got all the other American money. It's all right. You take it.'

I suppose I was getting paranoid. I took the money. Breaking the rules, Mr Tan called up to me that he had been told by the authorities that he was part of the pirate conspiracy. He seemed to think this was extremely funny. As time went on through May with Petroships still under suspicion and its representatives banned from the ship, he realised that it wasn't as amusing as he'd thought.

At 1.00 p.m. a member of the crew told me that a European was in a sampan alongside the ship on the side away from where the small tanker was still tied up, and wanted to talk to me. Thinking it might be Graham Pearce, I went to the rail at the appropriate spot and had a brief, shouted conversation over a distance of ten metres or so with a journalist named Andrew Bolt, who said he was from the Brisbane *Courier Mail*. I told him about the guards on the bridge and warned him that he might be shot at if spotted. I gave him the briefest of statements: that the reason I was being held was all to do with money and Chinese politics. When I got home and saw Linda's clipping file I learned a lot about the operations of some journalists.

I have to give Bolt credit for enterprise and gameness in getting out to the ship, but in writing up his report he let his imagination run away with him. About the only accurate material in his report is my claim that 'one side was playing off against another'. My language is not always polite, but I did not preface these remarks with, 'It's a f . . . . . . disgrace'. I did not ask him to contact Foreign Affairs in Australia. Why would I? I was already in touch with the consular people. I did not ask him to get a message to my wife. I certainly never used the word 'prisoner'. I talked about being a 'captive'. And I certainly never said, 'For God's sake, don't come on board or they'll shoot us all.'

There was no chance of Mr Bolt coming on board and equally no chance of a massacre. Another statement of Bolt's shows how he was improvising: 'The pirates stole his watch and then locked all twenty of the captives in their cabins'. I was hardly likely to worry about a watch; we were 21 not 20, and we were not locked in 'our' cabins. One headline in particular angered me when I saw it back in Australia: 'Get me out of here begs hijack captain.' At no time did I do any begging.

Bolt returned to the same spot the next day but I didn't see him as I was in a launch headed for shore. Apparently he waved at the launch. The guards on the ship spotted him and fired. This is how he reported it: 'The Chinese soldiers weren't mucking around. The first two shots went over my head. Then the guards on the captive tanker *Petro Ranger* aimed at me as I stood on the pitching fishing boat. I decided it was time to give up.'

I learned from the crew later that in fact a couple of shots were fired from weapons that were pointed to the sky. According to Bolt's reports the Chinese guards were 'dozing' aboard a patrol boat on the other side of the tanker. Not so. He says that I left the *Petro Ranger*, 'bursting around the stern', in a police launch before he was arrested. This is true, but his implication is that it had something to do with his visit. This is fantasy.

Bolt bled the story for all it was worth, or rather, all he could extract from it. He was held for a time and then deported. His account of his detention and the consequences makes pretty good reading:

> Eventually I was taken ashore to soldiers' headquarters. There a soldier waved copies of my interview with Captain Blyth from the morning's Australian papers in my face. 'Bad, bad, bad,' he shouted. I was kept under guard for 11 hours before being confronted by some senior officials.
>
> Could I sign a confession that I'd made up the entire story? No, I couldn't.
>
> Well, would I promise not to tell any lies? No worries.

Would I promise to leave Haikou the next day? Gosh, twist my arm.

And would I promise never to write another story about the amazing case of the *Petro Ranger* until they had finished their inquiry? Guess not.

Brave stuff, but the truth was very different. As it happened, I saw Bolt being frogmarched into the Marine Police headquarters when I was there on my business. Mr Li of the Chinese Foreign Office was there and he cracked a joke, 'The Captain might be free but the journalist is guilty.' Contrary to his account, Bolt signed an apology. Something he omits to mention is that he had entered China on a tourist rather than a journalist's visa and had not a leg to stand on. Under Chinese law, a foreign journalist was required to give fourteen days' notice before contacting interviewees. A Reuters report, quoting Mr Li saying that Bolt had signed a statement admitting that his story 'was seriously inconsistent with facts',[16] was true.

Bolt's irresponsible and inaccurate reports were faxed all around South-East Asian embassies and consulates and did a deal of damage. I would say that the hostility they aroused set relations between me and the Chinese officials back a certain distance. Denise, who was keeping a diary of developments by this stage, was informed of these communications and noted, 'Bolt's rubbish has screwed up Ken's prospects of release'. Luckily, Bolt was not believed. The Chinese who mattered knew me well enough by then to know that I would not have said the things Bolt reported.

Nevertheless, a consequence was that the Chinese, angered that their arrangements had been so easily circumscribed, stationed a patrol boat half a kilometre from the ship to make sure no other vessels could approach. The security had been screwed down even tighter.

13

'No needles!'

Except at night, there was always something happening aboard the *Petro Ranger*. Andrew Bolt was lucky he left when he did after his first visit, because hard on his heels the PSB arrived with their armed Marine Police escort to photograph the pirate's launch which was still lying on the ship's deck. Never in human history I'd guess would so many still photos have been taken of one speedboat. After a lot of shutter clicking, they departed.

I was convinced that some sort of power play was still going on between the Marine Police and the PSB. By this time the only evidence of the piracy left on the ship was the speedboat and the damage to my day room door.

With fewer visits from the officials and their accommodation clean and disinfected and our good cook doing his job, the spirits of the crew slowly began to rise. Although they were getting on together reasonably well, they had definitely fallen into national groups, the Malaysians spending most of their time together, the Indonesians doing the same and so on. The disgraced Malaysian officer was pretty much a pariah with only the Bangladeshis prepared to give him the time of day. It has to be said that the Bangladeshis were not popular with the others. At one point other crew members complained to me that a Bangladeshi officer had a pass key to the stores and the Bangladeshis were taking food at night. I confiscated the key and had the only Filipino aboard, an engine room fitter, weld metal blocks in place so that a heavy padlock could be put on the storeroom door. I gave the key to the cook. Small frictions like that are bound to develop in the sort of circumstances we were in, but if allowed to get out of hand can snowball into serious hostilities. I was always aware of friction between the Bangladeshis and the others and kept a close eye on it.

The novelty of the ride in the super fast speedboats had long since worn off. I was taken ashore to meet Graham Pearce, his wife and Mr Li yet again. I should mention that on these trips I always carried a plastic shopping bag. It contained toilet paper, which isn't widely available in China. In the headquarters building the toilet paper was last week's newspaper. Also in the bag were cigarettes for myself and for the obligatory exchanges and the pirates' documents about their next target which I'd collected. I never let those documents out of my sight.

The purpose of this meeting was to negotiate my coming ashore to live in a hotel with my wife *or* being allowed to leave China while the interminable investigation went on. Graham Pearce was pushing for this. There were two Commissars present at the meeting. They had the real overall authority but I wasn't quite aware of this at the time. Then another of those incidents that pointed up the cultural differences between westerners and Chinese occurred. I've had a lifelong habit of sprawling in any chair I sit in and putting my feet up on any convenient surface. My wife says there's never been a seat I couldn't turn into a lounge chair. It had been reported that, on occasions when I was in my day room with my shoes off and feet up on the desk, two guards had come in with some

The South China Sea. As you can see, by the time we reached Hainan Island, we had more than doubled our scheduled voyage.

A view of Haikou City from the harbour.

The *Petro Ranger* in Haikou Harbour.

The pirates' motor launch on board the *Petro Ranger*.

A view of the *Petro Ranger* taken from the bow.

The *Petro Ranger* taken from the Bridge.

Ship-to-ship transfer. Pictures 7, 8 and 9 show the *Petro Ranger* being unloaded in Haikou Harbour.

Unloading the *Petro Ranger*. You can just see Haikou City's skyline on the horizon.

Hainan Island is a favourite tourist destination in South-East Asia. Unfortunately, the circumstances did not allow me to appreciate the beauties of this island paradise.

GOLDEN COAST LAWTON HOTEL

金海岸羅頓大酒店

流光溢彩的"金海岸"外景
Brilliant outward appearance of the Golden Coast Lawton Hotel

Hainan, China
中國海南

The Golden Coast Lawton Hotel. 5-star service,
accommodation and surroundings.

request. I asked them to take their shoes off and no doubt was brusque with them. Referring to this, one of the Commissars said, 'Captain, do you realise what an insult it is in our society for you to sit with your feet raised like that?'

I wasn't in the mood for it. 'And do *you* realise,' I said, 'what an insult it is in my society for someone to hawk up from his guts and spit?' The Chinese spat continually. The guards thought nothing of spitting on the deck and indoors even the most senior and sophisticated officials spat into the waste paper baskets. My behaviour may appear ill-mannered, but it was not ill-considered. Chinese military personnel respect only confidence and strength and I was not about to back down to them on a question of etiquette.

Things didn't go smoothly at this meeting. At one point Daisy Pearce, who was interpreting, attempted to discover the names of the officials we were dealing with. She was given names but shook her head in despair.

'What's the matter?' I asked.

She laughed, 'These names they've given—if we were dealing in English they'd all be either Mr Smith or Mr Jones.'

After a lot of discussion the Commissars agreed that my wife could join me—but she would have to live with me on the ship. This wasn't acceptable to me. It was simply a way for the Chinese to use her for propaganda purposes, to show how humane and co-operative they were. Repeated requests from Graham Pearce for my wife and I to stay ashore had been refused. It was not a time for backing down.

'No,' I said. 'Unless we can live together ashore like civilised people, my wife will stay in Hong Kong.'

Again, this was misreported in the Australian newspapers as my refusal to accept a Chinese offer of living ashore and being 'joined by my family'. I was reported as 'opting' to remain on board. I'd have left the ship and lived in a hotel with Denise like a shot, but there was no such offer at this time. It looks as if the source for this nonsense may have been Mr Tan of Petroships which, significantly, was still representing itself as the ship's 'agent'.[17]

Most of the crew were still apprehensive about their futures. Only the Australian and Malaysian consular people had been active and the other nationalities were still 'non persons' as far as the Chinese were concerned until their passports and identities were confirmed. The Chinese appeared not to take the Malaysian Consul, who was dependent on his Australian counterpart for information, very seriously. By contrast, throughout my time in China, the Australian Ambassador in Beijing and his staff were in constant contact with the Chinese Foreign Office and were at all times energetic on my behalf.

At about ten o'clock the crew and I were put on one of the large patrol boats and taken ashore for a medical check. Here again, the difference in the Chinese attitude to me as a European compared to the predominantly Asian crew was very apparent. My officers and the crew had to stand in the fore part of the boat in the hot sun, whereas I was seated down near the stern under an awning. I was given tea and iced coconut water and the others were given nothing.

I remember remarking to the Bosun on the day of the hijacking that there were times when it was a disadvantage being a European and that this was one of them. Now I couldn't help reminding him of the comment and suggesting that now, in a different environment, the pendulum had swung my way. He took it in good part.

The hospital was within five minutes' walking distance of the wharf. I haven't a wide experience of hospitals; as I've said, I have a phobia about medical procedures, but I can honestly say that I've never seen a hospital like this one. The staff were sparkling clean in their persons and dress but the hospital itself and the equipment were both antiquated and filthy. Dogs walked around the place freely. The most remarkable feature was the smoking habits of the personnel; from the doctors on down they all smoked and heavily. I spent some time swapping cigarettes with doctors as they pressed 'Number one Chinese cigarettes' on me. It got to be like a smoking competition. Our medical consisted of an X-ray, ECG and blood pressure check.

The reports in the Australian media that we were charged $A50 each for these medical checks were not quite accurate. The fee was charged but, like all the other expenses connected with the Marine Police investigation, such as the fuel used for the launch trips, it was charged to Petroships. I knew this and didn't care. There was no chance of Petroships avoiding the account that was mounting up because the ship would not be cleared from Haikou until all bills were paid.

By lunch-time the medicals were completed and we were returned to the ship. In reality, this medical check was a sham. When I clapped eyes on the long table with syringes laid out and was told we would have to have cholera inoculations I refused on the grounds that we had all been vaccinated recently. Then they wanted to take blood samples, for what reason I wasn't told. I flatly refused. The crew looked very worried also but I assured them that no needles were going to be used. There was no way in the world I was going to submit to a needle that had been used God knows how many times before and was unlikely to have been sterilised.

'No,' I said. 'No needles.'

A heated argument followed but, as it turned out, there was no problem. As long as the fees were paid and the forms were filled in no one cared whether or not the medical procedures had actually been carried

体 格 检 查 表

姓 名	KENETH JOHN BLYTH		部职别					半身脱帽照片	
文化程度			诞生年月		籍贯				
既往病史									
家族病史								医院骑缝章	

								医师意见
五官科	眼	视 力	右 / 左	矫正视力	右 / 左	辨色力		
		砂眼	右 / 左	其它眼疾				
	耳	听力	右 公尺 / 左 公尺	耳疾				
	鼻	嗅觉		鼻及鼻窦疾病				
	咽喉							
	齿	龋齿		缺齿		齿槽脓漏		
	其它							签字

							医师意见
外科	身长	公分	胸围	公分	皮肤		
	体重	公斤	呼吸差	公分			
	淋巴		甲状腺		脊柱		
	四肢		关节		平底足		
	疝		肛门		生殖器		签字

6. A copy of the author's medical report (in Mandarin) from the examination carried out at Haikou Hospital.

内 科	血 压	110/70.	毫米水银柱		医师意见
	发育及营养状况	发育正常. 营养良好			正常.
	神经及精神	✓			
	肺及呼吸道	✓			
	心脏及血管	✓			
	腹部器官	. 正常	肝	肝肋下未及	签字 [签名]
			脾	脾肋下未触及	
	其 它				
化 验 检 查				化验员签字:	
胸部爱克斯线透 视	心.肺未见异常			医师签字: [签名]	
其 它 检 查	ECG: 正常			[签名]	
检 查 结 论	[签名]			负责医师 [签名] （盖章）	
检 查 医 院 意 见				[印章] 检查医院	（盖章）
备 注					

检查日期:　　　年　　月　　日

101

out. I signed, verifying that the blood tests had been done and the medics were appeased.

Sadly, apart from the cook who was permitted to go directly to the fresh food markets on one occasion, the rest of the crew saw only two things during their whole time in China: the jail inside what I had begun to call 'Gestapo Headquarters' and the hospital on a two-hour visit. The weather was good apart from occasional rain and it would have been humane for the men to have been allowed ashore to walk about a bit under supervision. This was never even discussed.

I took the opportunity of a quiet time the following day, with no disturbance from the officials, to quietly assess the crew and the effects the events to date had had on them. Things had definitely looked up. The crew had lost their fear of the Chinese guards stationed on the ship and had begun to share their food with them. I believe the Chinese enjoyed the different dishes as long as they were not too spicy. Rice, of course, was a staple with all of them. The crew had lost some of the strained, haggard look that had beset them, but they still had a long way to go before regaining their full mental health. I noted that they had problems sleeping and, although they all had their own individual cabins, they took to doubling up in the larger cabins or sleeping in twos and threes on the settees in the mess room. They preferred to live three or four to a cabin even if it meant sleeping on the deck for some of them. Through the Chief Officer, who spoke Indonesian and Malay, I tried to reassure them that they had nothing to fear but they still felt that there was safety in numbers.

I discovered a lot of cigarettes still in the bonded stores and distributed them to the crew free of cost, as I felt sure Petroships would be claiming the cost of them as an insurance item. By this stage I felt it was more important to lift the men's spirits a little than to stick to the rules.[18]

Oddly enough, my passion for the Glasgow Rangers football team led to me being on better terms with some of the Chinese guards and officials. As mentioned, as a youngster I had ambitions to play for the Rangers but my soccer skills weren't up to it. I always kept an up-to-date photograph of the team on the desk in my day room and in the 1997–98 season two famous international players, recognisable by soccer fans the world over—Brian Laudrup and Paul Gascoigne—were in the team. This photograph created a sensation among the soccer-mad Chinese. I couldn't speak Mandarin and only a few of them could speak very stilted English, but soccer proved to be an international language. If the Rangers' football manager could have seen us discussing and demonstrating tactics he would have been shocked or hysterical with laughter or both. It proved that soccer is truly a world game and can break down cultural barriers.

14

'Going ballistic'

My complaint that the matter had come down to a power play between the PSB and the Marine Police was born out by events over the next few days. The PSB came back on board, supposedly searching for evidence, but in fact they were just trying to demonstrate that they were still part of the investigation with the Marine Police. But all the evidence, apart from the pirates' launch, the damage to the communications room and my smashed door, had been documented or removed. I got so fed up with the PSB photographing my door (they had gone from still cameras to movie cameras to an elaborate TV camera) that I told them to unscrew the hinges and take it away with them as it would have to be replaced in Singapore anyway. They laughed and the door stayed.

At all times, these PSB officers when on the ship were accompanied by armed Marine Police, an interpreter and a soldier videoing the action. Somewhere in the Marine Police archives there must be many hours of these video tapes. They would not make very interesting viewing.

At four o'clock in the afternoon I went ashore again by launch (jacking up Petroships' fuel bill) to meet Graham Pearce, who was returning to Guangzhou in the morning, and a Chinese Foreign Office representative. Graham wanted to check if there was anything I needed and to let me use his cell phone to call Denise in Hong Kong. I took the opportunity to issue an ultimatum: I advised all parties that if my wife and I were not allowed to be together on shore to celebrate our silver wedding anniversary on the 17th (six days away) I was going to 'go ballistic'.

'Tell your Foreign Minister,' I said to the Chinese gentleman, 'and Graham, tell the Australian Ambassador in Beijing and our Foreign Minister in Canberra that I am not joking.'

I was at the end of my patience. It was, or should have been, clear to everyone that I could be of no further assistance to the Chinese authorities. The only reason for my detention was to keep me away from the western media for fear that I'd disclose what I knew and suspected about the involvement of elements of Chinese officialdom in the piracy. The Marine Police had completed their 'interrogation' of the pirate leader and surely had all the information they could get from him. In fact, he and the other pirates had been transferred to another jail as the Marine Police had no future use for them.

Back on the ship we managed to get the single side band radio working and for the first time since the drama began I contacted Petroships Singapore directly, only to find that they knew nothing about what was going on other than what Mr Tan could learn from Graham Pearce. I was advised that Mr Chan, the owner of Petroships and a Malaysian businessman who had a financial interest in the *Petro Ranger*, would be in Haikou within the next two days to meet with senior members of the Chinese Foreign Office who would be coming from Beijing. It was hoped that this meeting would resolve the impasse. I wasn't invited and I was asked to keep the information confidential, which I did. To this day I have no idea of whether these gentlemen actually came to Haikou or whether the meeting ever took place. I saw no evidence of it.

Another three machetes were found by the PSB along with a dagger and some balaclavas. I feel pretty sure that these items were left by the Marine Police for the PSB to find as a face-saving gesture. Still attending to detail and with time no object, the Marine Police took the Chief Officer and the radio operator, who had had to assist the pirates with cargo work and communications, ashore to be interviewed again before finally signing their statements.

That evening, when I was strolling around the ship, I talked to some of the guards (using Saini as an interpreter) and asked them for a closer look at their machine pistols, noting that they appeared to be of a fairly small calibre.

I said to the senior guard, 'With a small calibre like that the gun wouldn't be accurate for a target 100 metres away.'

He pointed. 'Captain, how far is it from here to the bow?'

'One hundred and two metres.'

He smiled. 'Captain, you go up there and I'll shoot at you. If I miss, you'll be proved right.'

Also smiling, I refused his offer. He obviously knew more about guns than I did.

This sort of banter shows that not only were the crew and I becoming bored by the slowness of proceedings, but that the guards were also finding it tedious and were glad of any distraction.

On Friday 15 May at 4.00 p.m. I went ashore in a powerboat and, on entering 'Gestapo Headquarters', was taken to a large, subdivided conference room. In the first section were Mr Tan and Captain Jerries of Petroships, but I was ushered past them to the second section where for the first time I met Ms Ann Giles, Vice-Consul from the Australian Consulate in Guangzhou, and her assistant and interpreter, Sophia, a Chinese woman. Both were in their early thirties and wore short skirts. Civilisation at long last!

This was when I learned, from Sophia, of the identity and authority of the Commissar who I'd known to be a senior officer; but I hadn't been aware of quite how senior he was. She advised me only to deal with him as he had the ultimate authority to make final and binding decisions. There was an obvious air of excitement which communicated itself to me when Ann Giles told me that on Saturday I was to be released to a hotel for the rest of my stay in China. Arrangements were being made for my wife to catch a flight to Haikou the next morning and we could stay together, *but* only if I signed an agreement with the following six conditions:

1   I was not allowed to leave the hotel without the permission of the Marine Police.

2   I was to have no contact with Petroships or the media.

3   The only telephone calls I could make or receive were to the Australian Consulate, the Marine Police, the Chinese Foreign Office and my daughters in Australia.

4   Although I was to stay in a hotel I, and not Petroships, was to be held responsible for the ship. I was to visit it twice a week and verify that all was well; or in the event of an emergency or when directed to do so by the Chinese authorities.

5   My wife had to undertake not to speak with Petroships or the media.

6   The final condition was that the Marine Police nominated the hotel. (This was fine by me as the one they chose was a five-star establishment, the Golden Coast Lawnton Hotel. I felt as if I'd gone from the doghouse to the penthouse and, when

installed in the hotel the next day, I discovered that our suite virtually *was* the penthouse.)

I signed the agreement willingly and it was taken and shown to Mr Tan, who started to complain about the terms, particularly at having no contact with me or access to the ship. But when the Commissar ordered him to stop he stopped. Having already been thrown down the steps he'd learned his lesson. An important man he may have been in Singapore, but he clearly didn't count for much in Haikou.

And so within one hour all the arrangements were in place. After handshakes all round with the Commissar, his officers and the Vice-Consul, it was back onto the launch to spend my last night aboard the *Petro Ranger*.

I gave the crew my last few bits of clothing and split the remaining cigarettes up among them. By this time the crew were on good terms with the Chinese guards, who themselves were sick of the long spells of duty aboard the ship and missing out on their normal eight-hour day and social life. Consequently, the crew had no fear of them. I assured them that I'd be back regularly and in a few days I'd bring my wife to meet them all. I felt she should meet the men who'd shared the hardships with me. The crew were grateful that I'd stood up to the Chinese guards and had never let them put a foot wrong or cause the crew any trouble. Given the attitude of the Chinese, it's unlikely that an Asian captain could have achieved this and the crew knew it.

The excitement began to build. Arrangements had been made for the Vice-Consul and a representative from the Chinese Foreign Office to meet Denise at the airport. Our actual reunion would take place at Marine Police headquarters, not the most congenial place I thought at the time, but I didn't care. After almost five weeks of continual stress, it was an immense relief to know that the ordeal was coming to an end.

15

The Golden Coast
Lawnton Hotel

In the mid-morning a launch took me to the headquarters building to wait for Denise. It was the only time I went to the sixth and highest floor, and the conference room I was shown into was palatial—equal to any boardroom in a big, prosperous company. I was given tea and told I'd have a 30-minute wait. The officers who dealt with me at this time I had not seen before and did not see again. They appeared to be of a very superior type and treated me with extreme courtesy.

Denise had been taken first to the hotel, which was about fifteen minutes' drive away, by Ann Giles and Sophia. She checked in and left her luggage there. Mr Li from the Chinese Foreign Office, who I'd now met so many times, met them there and they were taken to headquarters. At about 11.00 a.m. Denise and I were finally reunited.

It's difficult to convey the feelings we had at that moment. I had been away from home for four and a half months and for a twelve-day period within the last month Denise hadn't known for certain whether she was a wife or a widow. And I'd had moments of wondering whether I'd ever see her and our daughters again. I suspect that only people returning from dangerous military service could have similar emotions.

We were left quite alone for about five minutes which was precisely the right thing to have done given the way we felt.

Whatever difficulties and frustrations I might have experienced at the hands of the Chinese, I have to say that everyone, at all levels, treated Denise with the utmost courtesy. They met her on all occasions in a friendly fashion, were unfailingly helpful and, when she showed an interest, they tried to explain their customs and traditions. They were proud of Hainan Island.

So, after a short period alone, it was into two cars* and off to the hotel. Only certain members of the hotel staff knew exactly who we were and there was a brief panic when, on showing my passport, it became apparent that I didn't have an entry visa. I had to smile; there were no entry visas available for the way in which I'd entered China. Between them the Chinese Foreign Office people and the Marine Police sorted it out and attended to the paperwork. We were shown to our suite, the Chinese and the Australian consulate people departed and we were left alone for the rest of the day.

I had asked Denise to bring some clothes for me as all I had to wear were two white boiler suits and a khaki uniform. In fact, she brought a suitcase of clothes and a watch. (I never got back the one the pirates stole on that first night.) The clothes hung loosely on me because I had lost a good deal of weight through the ordeal and I am of a lean build anyway. Only much later did Denise reveal to me the shock she'd received on first seeing me. Normally, I have a fresh, tanned appearance but now I had sunken eyes, hollow cheeks and a pallid complexion. Simple things like a good, hot shower, clean clothes and well-prepared western food were like manna from heaven. Just enjoying and getting

---

*   It is interesting to note that the drivers of the cars were very uncomfortable at having to wait outside 'Gestapo Headquarters' and, in fact, had to be coerced into doing so by Mr Li.

used to these conditions, and getting lots of sleep, took up that first day. Denise filled me in on the extensive media coverage she'd been following and I was astonished to learn just how much had been written about the hijacking. When I later reviewed it I was equally surprised to find how inaccurate it was, both about the piracy and the intrigue surrounding our detention in China. But for now I simply luxuriated in the pleasure of being reunited with my wife in such pleasant surroundings.

At such times I suppose your body and metabolism dictate your behaviour. I slept long and often which suggests that until then my sleep had been shallow and not restful. It amuses me to recall that, for my first meal in the hotel, I had a passion for a hamburger. I called room service and ordered two hamburgers and a chef's salad, which seemed like a modest meal. Up came an enormous platter with a magnificent fresh salad complete with bacon and croutons and two sumptuous hamburgers with French fries. I hoed in, demolished most of the salad and my hamburger and fries. Denise had eaten some salad and fries and picked at the hamburger.

'You don't want it?' I asked. 'Give it here.' I ate her hamburger and cleaned up the fries. I had already eaten a good few of the bananas from the fruit bowl that was renewed daily. I'm not a glutton; looking back I realise that my body was asking for something that it needed.

A couple's silver wedding anniversary is supposed to be a very special day, to be celebrated with family and friends in a setting selected by the couple.[19] There are usually cards, gifts and speeches. Denise and I had none of that, but our celebration was unique; I doubt that the circumstances could ever be duplicated.

Our day started with a quiet breakfast in the main lobby coffee room. On returning to our suite, we were greeted by Ann Giles, who presented us with two huge bouquets of flowers: one from the Australian Ambassador and his staff in Beijing and the other from Ms Zena Armstrong, the Consul General in Guangzhou and her staff. We were deeply appreciative and in a way this very thoughtful gesture was in keeping with the strenuous efforts the diplomatic people had made on our behalf, unlike some other branches of government.

After Denise had left for Hong Kong (which the media didn't know) and my older daughter had returned to RAAF Edinburgh, matters reached a point when, prior to going to work, my younger daughter innocently answered the front door only to be confronted by two journalists who informed her that, if they didn't get a background story on me they would simply make it up. I have never sought out these journalists, but cannot predict how I would react to them if ever we meet.

When I learned of these events from Denise, one of the first things I did was to phone my younger daughter and tell her to phone Harry M. Miller and request he handle all media affairs. I am glad to say he happily agreed to do this and, after an appropriate press release was issued by Harry M. Miller, the media tended to behave better.

Ann Giles left for her flight to Guangzhou. The highlight of the day for me was finally being able to telephone my older daughter, Wendy, with whom I'd had no contact since the start of the affair. Like her mother and sister, she'd spent a period wondering if I were dead or alive and had suffered some media harassment. This call gave me the feeling that, although we were continents apart, in a way we were all together as a close family.

After a light lunch, I slept until about five o'clock when we both showered and dressed in the best clothes available to us and set off for one of the five restaurants in the hotel. The maître d'hôtel spoke perfect English with an American accent and had obviously been waiting for us to make our appearance. He guided us to the main restaurant, which he said was the most appropriate for our special occasion. The food was set out buffet style and our host explained all the ingredients and cooking styles of the innumerable dishes. The service was magnificent; a young woman was on hand to light my cigarettes and to provide a clean ashtray after I'd finished each cigarette. The food was delicious. A drinks waiter arrived early in the piece with a litre bottle of Johnny Walker Black Label and my glass was constantly being topped up. I'd had no alcohol since signing my current contract. In fact, my last drink before that night had been on Boxing Day 1997. By the end of the evening I was operating on automatic pilot. Fortunately, Denise doesn't drink.

I'm quite sure that some of the waiters and attendants were security people of some kind, there to make sure we weren't disturbed; but this in no way detracted from our enjoyment. It was a wonderful evening with our every wish catered for. Topped up with good food and Black Label, I have no precise idea of when this splendid occasion came to an end.

16

Out of the loop

It was now clear that the Chinese authorities, the Marine Police and the PSB had moved into the next phase of their agenda: negotiating with Petroships and its representatives as to how to finalise the affair to the benefit of all parties. The crew, the pirates and myself were now effectively out of the loop having told everything we knew. From here on it was simply a matter of wheeling and dealing at the highest levels, which inevitably involved corruption and political manoeuvring as the bargaining went on.

My chief regret was that the crew were now denied any shore visits. The only reason the Malaysians had been ashore was to meet with their consul, who had only paid perfunctory visits, coinciding with when the Australian consular people were seeing me. As the ship was registered in Malaysia he was theoretically involved, but all his moves appeared to be token gestures only.[20] As far as I know he was unable to assist his seven nationals in gaining access to a mobile phone or in contacting their families. In part, he was stymied by the indifference, even contempt, shown him by the Chinese who saw Malaysia as irrelevant. They, rightly, took the view that the ship was owned by a Singaporean company and that the buck stopped there.

It's a pity this line of reasoning was not followed through.

At 5.00 p.m. on Monday 18 May, a day I mainly spent sleeping, eating, exploring the hotel complex and trying to contain my impatience to be out of this maze, I was visited by the Commissar and his interpreter.

This threw us into a total panic as at that time I was sitting at the large desk in our suite drafting out a covering letter to accompany the documents for the MT *Surin*, the vessel scheduled to be hijacked after the *Petro Ranger*. I planned to give this letter and the documents to Graham Pearce on our next meeting for him to send through official channels to DFAT in Canberra. I imagined that this could spark an immediate enquiry, with the cooperation of Malaysia and Singapore.[21] Such an enquiry would have brought a great deal of solid evidence to light.

My immediate concern was to get the documents out of sight of the Commissar. As Denise was ushering them in, I pretended to be straightening out the quilt on the bed but in fact I was shoving the papers under it and out of sight. To have been found in possession of these papers would have been disastrous. It could easily be made to look as if I was a party to the syndicate's operations. I think my James Bondish action in taking, concealing and handing over these documents greatly contributed to the strain I was under through this part of the ordeal and, probably, to my weight loss (see Appendix A).

'Are you and your wife comfortable, Captain? Is everything okay?' the Commissar asked.

I assured him that we were fine. In a conversation that followed, he asked me if I had ever heard of a Mr Wong in connection with Petroships.

'I know there is a Mr Ong in Petroships' Chartering Department,' I said. 'But I don't know of a Mr Wong.'[22]

He nodded in what I suppose has to be called an enigmatic fashion and passed on to something else. As

I see things now, what the Commissar's question revealed was that the Chinese Marine Police, through their interrogation of Herman and other investigations, had extracted all the details of the Chinese and Singaporean ends of the syndicate's operations. In short they, and they alone, knew the whole story.

The interview or discussion or whatever it might be called ended but not without another of those odd slips of communication between east and west. The Commissar's interpreter was a young woman, about the same age, I guessed, as Wendy. Quite innocently, I asked how old she was.

'You are not permitted to ask that question, Captain,' was the reply.

The next day Denise and I took a chance. Ignoring the signed undertaking, we ventured out of the hotel where we were feeling distinctly cooped up. There were no other westerners in the place at that time and although the staff were all kind and courteous, there is a sort of forced formality to such contact which quickly becomes tedious. So we snuck out and went for a one-hour walk through the nearby stalls and shops that represented the true face of China rather than the five-star facade built for the most affluent Chinese and, of course, visitors from the West. I bought a wallet from one of the vendors because my own wallet had been taken by the pirates. Who knows where it is now. In a minor way, this expedition felt like regaining some sense of independence although, in truth, what I still mostly wanted to do at this time was eat and sleep.

Our rule-breaking apparently went unnoticed or was ignored. The next day I was advised that the following day a car from Marine Police headquarters would take me to the dock to catch a launch at 9.00 a.m. out to the ship to make my inspection. I called the Australian Consul in Guangzhou to see if there had been any further developments. There hadn't been. My opinion was confirmed that the only reason the Chinese were holding on to me was to prevent me speaking to the media in case something I said might interfere with finalising whatever deal Petroships and the Chinese were working on. Graham Pearce was due back in Haikou the next day so I'd have support if there were new arrangements to be coped with.

At issue was the money the Marine Police had recovered from the pirates and the balance of the cargo which had a value of around $A1.75 million. Graham Pearce and I had talked this over earlier. Neither of us had any doubts that the Chinese were going to keep the fuel.

'I wonder how they're going to do it?' Graham had said.

I'd been carrying marine cargoes long enough to have some idea. 'Evidence,' I suggested. 'They could hang onto it as evidence.'

And so it turned out. When I arrived at headquarters on Thursday 21 May, I had a brief meeting with two officers and an interpreter. I was advised that an agreement had been reached with Petroships regarding the release of the ship. The Marine Police and PSB had the company's permission to discharge the balance of the cargo to be kept in shore tanks as 'evidence' pending a court case into the piracy. The money from the sale of the 5000 tonnes of diesel would also be retained as 'evidence'. This was to happen on the Saturday and I would have to be present to witness the discharge and sign the inevitable documents. Some representatives from Petroships, including their lawyer, would also be present. It would be the first time anyone connected with the company would be allowed on board the ship.

I went out to the ship to check that all was well. The Chinese guards had been changed since I'd left and only a few of the original soldiers still remained. But the crew and the soldiers were on good terms by now and there was a relaxed atmosphere at last aboard the *Petro Ranger*. The Chief Officer had kept the accommodation spotlessly clean but the Chinese would not allow any maintenance to be done outside on deck and there important maintenance procedures had not been carried out. The crew, although over the worst of their fears, were very disappointed to learn that they would not be flown back to Singapore as they had hoped, but would have to take the ship back under the command of Captain Jerries, whom for many reasons they disliked.

Unfortunately, it has been my experience that many ships' captains from underdeveloped countries do not treat their crews well. For reasons I don't understand, they seem to take their position of authority as a chance to exploit their own people. Captain Jerries, a Singaporean of Sri Lankan ancestry, was a well-educated but chip-on-the shoulder kind of man, possibly uncomfortable working for the ethnic Chinese Singaporean firm. His style was harsh and confrontational and I feared that the crew would have a trying time on the voyage to Singapore. But there was nothing I could do about it. I did take ashore a bag of letters from the crew and made certain they were correctly posted to the men's families from the hotel. It was something; but people who'd been through what they had and, with one notable exception, had behaved well, deserved better.

China is a strange place. Expect the unexpected is what I would advise a visitor. I should have gone ashore at 3.00 p.m. and returned to the hotel, but the soldiers told me that there was no boat available. This was a ploy. What actually happened was that they delayed me so that Lieutenant Pei An Li, who I'm pretty sure had received a promotion, could get out to the ship with a case of Chinese beer and we could share a comradely drink.

What with one thing and another, I didn't get ashore until 8.20 p.m. and I was promptly arrested on the dock as the night duty officer had no idea who I was. The soldiers from the ship explained matters and a utility with a sergeant as driver was quickly supplied to take me back to the hotel. The sergeant insisted that we stop for a drink at one of the little bars along the way and, not wanting to be disobliging, I agreed. Although I'd phoned Denise at 8.20 to tell her I was running late, it was considerably later still when I got back to the hotel. The Chinese Foreign Office people, always keeping close tabs on me, had begun to worry about where I was and Denise was not at all pleased. But I managed to smooth down all feathers and so this day, which seemed to be pointing towards a finish to all the chess board moves, came to a quiet end.

17

The Chinese 'Wild West'

At 10.00 a.m. Denise met Graham Pearce and Daisy for the first time. During this visit I gave him the MT *Surin* documents and the covering letter. Half an hour later a Marine Police officer arrived and then Phillip Ng from Petroships showed up. He was an engineer and the only person available from the company who spoke Mandarin as Mr Tan had had to return to Singapore to bring back the documents which the PSB required in order to release the ship.

The head of the PSB arrived to confirm that all was in order and the Pearces and the Blyths had lunch together in one of the hotel's excellent restaurants. Graham and Daisy were only in Haikou for the day, specifically to check that all went smoothly and to confer with their counterparts from the Chinese Foreign Office.

After lunch Denise and I went to headquarters and met Phillip Ng and the Petroships lawyer, a Ms Ho. We had a wait of over an hour while the PSB waited for a certain document to be faxed from Petroships. The fax arrived and a furious argument broke out when Ms Ho demanded a copy. Apparently it was Petroships' understanding that the PSB were to provide them with some documents when this fax arrived. The PSB didn't comply. Nevertheless, in the mid-afternoon we set off for the ship by powerboat accompanied by three Marine Police officers.

It's a bizarre feature of all this coming and going between ship and shore that there was no vessel identifiable as the *Petro Ranger* to be seen. My ship still carried the name *Wilby* as painted by the pirates on the bow and the stern.

On all previous occasions getting from the ship to the launch had been simply a matter of hopping down onto the small tanker moored alongside, crossing to the other side and stepping down onto the launch. But now that tanker had been taken away and things were different. It was a considerable distance from the launch up to the deck of the ship and the only way to negotiate it was by climbing up a rope ladder (the 'pilot's ladder'). Ms Ho was frankly terrified, but I went up behind her, promising to catch her if she fell. It was no easy matter for Denise either but she made it, greatly to the relief of the Chinese who, I later learned, had dreaded the consequences if the wife of 'Mister Captain' fell.

Denise met most of the crew, including Saini and Benny who I'd told her about. They appreciated her visit although they tended to be shy and didn't have much to say. After all they'd been through, a simple thing like that, meeting the Captain's wife, meant a lot to them. They and the Chinese guards were very kind and respectful towards her and she enjoyed the visit.

A small tanker came out from Haikou and within an hour, after calculating exactly how much cargo was left on board, we started to discharge approximately 1000 tonnes of the remaining diesel. Denise took photographs of the discharge. It was about 8.30 p.m. when this operation was completed and the Marine Police officer in charge told us we could all travel back to Haikou on the tanker. This trip took about an hour and, under different circumstances it would have been pleasant. It was a beautiful evening and the city's lights growing larger and brighter as we neared shore were an impressive sight.

Expect the unexpected. It was close to ten o'clock when we berthed at a small wharf, which was in pitch darkness. The Marine Police officer told us just to follow the fuel pipe through the scrub until we got to the main highway and then hail cabs to get us back to our hotels. This was a big change from the careful shepherding I'd received up to that time. After stumbling through the unlit scrub for about fifteen minutes, cursing and swearing as we went, we reached the highway where we all burst into laughter at the absurdity of it. Ms Ho was able to explain our plight to a couple of cab drivers and so we got back to the hotel. During our trip in the cab, we were escorted by many young Chinese on their mopeds. We waved to them and, seeing a European woman in the cab, they gave Denise more wolf whistles I'm sure than she'd ever received before.

It was about this time that Graham Pearce came up with the best description of southern China. 'It's like the wild west of America in the 1860s,' he said. 'People make up their own laws, especially the army.'[23]

It was very evident now that the whole affair had come down to a question of money. I'd been told that it was okay for me to meet with representatives of Petroships if I wished, so the deal must have been set. I was about to gain an insight into how things were sometimes done in this part of the world.

Graham Pearce phoned to say he hoped that we would be out of China by the 28th. I phoned my daughters and let them know we hoped to be home by the end of the month. There seemed to be more hoping than firm action going on. Denise was unwell one day and on another I had a haircut. We felt as if we were filling in time which could have been much better spent. Denise had to apply for an extension to her entry visa (not a hopeful sign) and I had to get an exit visa, which was more positive. Graham Pearce took these matters in hand.

On Tuesday 26 May, I was taken to headquarters and told to go to the ship and move it to a small wharf about two hours down the coast.

'No,' I said. 'Absolutely not.'

'Why not, Captain?'

I told the Marine Police I had done everything possible to assist them in their investigation of the piracy, had met all their requirements, signed their documents, complied with their restrictions on my liberty,[24] but I would not, under any circumstances, participate in what was being done now. I was given a long, hard stare.

'Very well, Captain. Captain Jerries will do it.'

I shrugged. Where the rest of the fuel was unloaded I have no idea as I refused to have anything further to do with the ship until it became time for me to sign documents prior to its departure for Singapore. My recalcitrance was accepted with no obvious ill will by the Marine Police, but Petroships were unhappy with my attitude. However, there was nothing they could do about it.

All in all, this was a very tense time for Denise and myself and after six weeks of strain and nervous tension I was in no mood for bureaucratic bungling and delay, still less for obvious wheeler-dealing. On the 26th a Mr Joung from the Chinese Foreign Affairs Department collected Denise at 2.30 p.m. and took her to the main PSB office to get her visa extended. The extension for a month cost $US15, pricey enough, but Denise did not arrive back at the hotel until 5.20 p.m. This simple procedure took almost three hours and, as every traveller knows, waiting without having any idea of what is causing the delay is stressful.

No one would, or could, give us any hard information as to what was intended, neither the Chinese

Foreign Office nor the Australian Consulate. My nerves were frayed. Graham Pearce and his wife arrived from Guangzhou and declared their intention to stay in Haikou until the Chinese allowed us to depart. This was some comfort but the bureaucratic grind went on and on. At 4.00 p.m. the next day (why not earlier I never discovered), the same young woman interpreter who had rebuked me for asking her age called at the hotel to take me to headquarters to sign a statement I had made on 1 May, which seemed like a lifetime ago. Interestingly, like something from the past, when you sign Chinese documents such as this, you have to make a red ink imprint with your thumb first and sign over that. Of course, that gives the officials a finger-print, so it may not be so old-fashioned after all.

On the way back to the hotel she said, 'Captain, you wanted to know how old I was?'

I said, 'Yes, because I thought you looked about the same age as my older daughter.'

'Captain,' she said with a beautiful smile. 'I am 24 years of age.'

Pondering this, I thought, *They're the same age and both serving their countries, yet how different their worlds are.*

When I got back to my room Graham Pearce rang with a suggestion that we all meet in the bar for a drink. *All* meant Denise and myself, him and his wife, and Phillip Ng and Captain Jerries from Petroships, now that company people were allowed to associate with me. This meeting was to mark the fact that the *Petro Ranger* was being released the next day and that Denise and myself would be free to fly to Singapore the day after that.

Unfortunately, whether he was bitter about having to take the ship back to Singapore or was unhappy about having had to take part in the unloading of the fuel or had some other grievance, Captain Jerries, after one beer, behaved insultingly towards the Pearces and my wife and me. I excused myself, went to my room and called Kenneth Kee, the managing director of Petroships. I described Jerries' behaviour and Mr Kee immediately called Jerries on his cell phone. The result of this call was that Jerries and Phillip Ng left.

So the Blyths and the Pearces spent a pleasant night together over good wine and food. During the evening the PSB's senior officer met with us to collect my passport for the issuing of an exit visa.

'It will be returned in the morning, Captain.'

18

The *Petro Ranger* aka the MT *Wilby*

Six weeks after the seizure of the *Petro Ranger* by the pirates, the ship was finally to be released and able to be returned to Singapore.[25] But not before Petroships supplied documentation worded exactly as the PSB required, and which had to be delivered to them by hand by Mr Tan, the executive director of the company. Rumours had been circulated by Petroships' representatives that the PSB wanted documents notarised by the Singapore government, but this was nonsense.[26]

I spent the morning quietly in the hotel with Graham Pearce, who was in constant contact with the Chinese Foreign Affairs Office in Haikou, DFAT in Canberra and the Consul General in Guangzhou. I hate to think what the cost in cell phone calls throughout the affair would have been. It was an apprehensive time for all of us. Anyone with experience of China would understand our attitude, because in China what is supposed to happen and what actually happens can be very different things.

The Marine Police had phoned in the morning and requested that I be at Headquarters at 2.45 p.m. as all parties were going out to the ship on one of the large patrol boats at 3 p.m. My role was to verify that all the ship's documents that had been taken ashore during their investigation had been returned and were in correct order as these papers are required to be carried on every merchant ship and produced for the authorities every time a ship enters a port anywhere in the world.

I asked if my wife and Daisy Pearce could join us and this was initially agreed to by the Marine Police, but around noon I got a call from the PSB withdrawing this permission. At the time I thought this was sheer obstructionist bastardry, but it later became clear that the authorities wanted as few Australian witnesses to the document signing as possible.

As arranged, I presented myself at headquarters and the party assembled: Mr Tan, Captain Jerries, Ms Ho, some Marine Police officers plus the Commissar and the Colonel I had not seen in the past four weeks and Mr Li of the Chinese Foreign Office. And there were also the PSB officers who I viewed with distaste as being completely corrupt. For the last time I made the trip out to the *Petro Ranger*, still bearing the pirate name, *Wilby*.

By late May the weather is warm in Hainan and to my surprise I was escorted to a large stateroom on the patrol boat where I was joined by the Marine Police Colonel and his staff, the Commissar and his people and Mr Li. The rest of the company had to stand out on the deck in the hot sun. There was no love lost between the Marine Police and the PSB and this was evident in their attitudes and body language. Although the Petroships representatives were tolerated, they were basically treated with undisguised contempt by the Marine Police.

I had a chance then to speak privately to the Colonel using Mr Li as an interpreter. I apologised for my unintended rudeness at our first meeting. He replied that he understood that I had been very tired at the time and had just come through a very stressful period. Smiling, he asked if the hotel he had selected was to my liking.

'It's excellent, Colonel,' I replied. 'We could not have hoped for better.'

Still smiling, he said, 'I picked it not only because of its quality and because I knew you would get the rest you needed there, but because I could keep an eye on your safety. My office is directly across the road.'

That explained something Denise and I had noticed and wondered about: why two apparently elite troops always stood guard at the narrow entrance to a compound directly opposite the hotel. The Chinese government had apparently guaranteed our safety while in its territory and the Colonel was taking no chances. Also, keeping an eye on us meant keeping us clear of the dubious negotiations going on between the PSB and Petroships.

On arrival at the ship we immediately made our way to the cargo control room which had a table big enough to accommodate all parties and the documents. The atmosphere was tense with the Petroships people desperately concerned that nothing should go wrong and the hostility between the Marine Police and the PSB thick enough to cut with a knife. I checked that all the documents—basically receipts for items taken from the ship and returned—were in order and signed. One point puzzled me: as well as signing for the ship's documents in its true name, I was also required to sign, on behalf of Petroships, for the ship's papers in the name MT *Wilby*. I naively assumed that the Chinese had no further use for them in their proceedings against the pirates and that they were being returned to Petroships to assist in what I expected to be subsequent investigations by the Singapore and Malaysian authorities. I was wrong. It was not until much later that I discovered the real significance of returning the *Wilby* papers to Petroships (see page 140).

This signing session took about fifteen minutes with the last item being a document showing that the Chinese and the ship's figures on the amount of fuel discharged at Haikou were virtually the same. A short photographic session followed and then all were free to depart, or so I thought.

The ship was leaving for Singapore immediately and I formally handed over control to Captain Jerries, who was on his best behaviour. I suppose my manner towards him could have been described as cool. Then the immigration authorities returned my passport with the exit permit stamped in it. The port/immigration authorities had joined us by this time and, after checking that the ship's and crew's documents were all in order, gave Captain Jerries a clearance. This meant that the ship could depart still bearing the name *Wilby*, which I thought odd. The immigration authorities explained that I would be flying out the following day and would need to go to the PSB office to have a retrospective entry visa stamped in my passport as I would need evidence of both entry and exit at the airport.

Just after the photographic session, I farewelled the crew, which was an emotional moment. They gathered as a group, thanked me for what I'd done for them and several said they'd never forget me. There were a few tears in a few eyes. Strangely enough, some of the Chinese guards thanked me for my action in escaping to them as I had, because they had come out prepared to take over the ship and, as they believed the pirates still to be armed, they feared that there would have been bloodshed.

When the time came for a group photograph to include the crew, the Chinese officials and Petroships representatives, Saini was found to be missing. Eventually he made it back in time and I discovered what had happened. Through his ability to speak Mandarin he'd built up a good rapport with some of the soldiers and they'd smuggled him ashore for a drinking session to celebrate his birthday. Being something of a larrikin he'd got rather drunk, but we all agreed to record his reason for being ashore as 'immediate medical attention'.

With everything settled, the Colonel, the Commissar, Mr Li and I left in a powerboat. A thoughtful man, the Colonel asked if I'd liked to circle the ship and I said I would. We circled her for one last time and I could see that the crew had begun to paint out *Wilby* and substitute the real name of the ship. She was leaving immediately and it's worth noting that this is another example of the loose way of things in southern China—this voyage was quite illegal under maritime law because the radio equipment on the ship wasn't functioning. I didn't say anything; the last thing I wanted was a glitch at this point.

Arriving at the dock, I said goodbye to the Colonel. I never learned his name. At headquarters Mr Li asked me to return to Hainan on holiday some time and not to judge China by the extraordinary four weeks I'd spent there amid intrigue and worse. Mr Li arranged transport across the city to an office where my passport was stamped with an entry permit. Back at the hotel I learned that Graham Pearce had booked flights for us: 9.40 a.m. by Dragonair to Hong Kong and then a Singapore Airlines flight down to Singapore.

After a light meal shared with the Pearces it was back to the room to pack and to phone Linda and Wendy to let them know we'd be home within a few days. We spent our last night in China still troubled by the lingering thought: *Will anything else change before we leave, or is this really it?*

We were up at 6.00 a.m. and after an early breakfast the hotel provided transport to the airport for the Pearces and ourselves. It was gratifying to leave such a fine hotel where we'd been very well looked after without having to pay a cent. With a glint in his eye, the Commissar had assured me that Petroships would be footing all bills. On the drive to the airport I had a sneaking feeling that this was all going too smoothly.

After paying our departure tax we said goodbye and thanked the Pearces for all their help and kindness and set off to the immigration counter to have our passports checked prior to our passing through to the departure lounge. Denise went through without trouble but panic broke out when I presented my passport.

'Captain, your entry permit is not on our computer.'

'Look, it's stamped in the passport.'

'It is not on our computer.'

I could hardly believe it. Another flurry of phone calls by Graham Pearce, recalled for one last piece of help, to the Chinese Foreign Affairs office and the matter was sorted out. It appears that an interservice basketball game had been on when I had the stamp put in the passport and the computer entry hadn't been made.

At 9.25 a.m. our flight was called and it was out onto the tarmac to board the 737. The doors closed almost immediately and we were down the runway and airborne at 9.47 a.m. I must have been checking my watch minute by minute to recall the time with this precision, still fearful that something would go wrong. I was overwhelmed by a feeling of relief when I heard the aircraft's wheels lock into place as we climbed to our cruise height. I hadn't realised how much stress I'd been under, day by day for six weeks, until that moment. I felt as if I was now, suddenly, living in a different world.

19

'Thank you'

The flight to Hong Kong took only 50 minutes and
after baggage transfers we had a two-hour wait and
then took off for Singapore, that leg taking about
three-and-a-half hours. So I was finally out of Chinese
territory where I hadn't wanted to be in the first place.
It was an odd feeling to be back where I'd left from
all that time ago and knowing that I could more or
less do what I liked, go wherever I wanted. There was
an air of unreality about it.

On arrival at Changi terminal 2, we were met by
Captain Johnny Liew and another Superintendent from
Petroships, an Australian consular officer and two security men from the Singapore police. They took our
passports and baggage tags and we were whisked off
on the monorail that joins the two Changi terminals.
We went to terminal 1, then down into a car and back
to terminal 2, had our passports and baggage tags
returned to us and were driven off. It was all very
confusing, but apparently western TV and news cameras and journalists had been waiting for us so we'd
been taken on this mystery tour to avoid them.

In the car to the hotel, for some inexplicable reason,
the main topic of conversation from the Petroships
people was their use of a clairvoyant in the early stages

of the affair. I was shown his drawings and notes (see Chapter 6). I found this weird. Of course, at this stage I had no idea of what had gone on in the initial stages of the search and, with everything that had happened, had given no thought to it. I had assumed that the Singaporean and Malaysian navies and air forces had been out searching for us from day one. Wrong. In reality, the Singaporean government had decided it was a Malaysian problem given that the ship was registered there. The buck was quickly passed.

After arrival at the hotel we were given an hour to freshen up and then we were due to meet over dinner with Mr Alan Chan, the owner of Petroships, Mr Kenneth Kee, the Managing Director of Petroships, the Australian Defence Adviser to Singapore and Brunei and his wife, another consular official from the Australian High Commission and Captain Liew. To be frank, this was the last thing I wanted to do. We were both tired and would have preferred a quiet night to adjust to the new freedom, but we felt obliged to agree. The setting in the New Plaza building was delightful and the meal was both delicate and delicious but I was 'out on my feet' and I don't recall much of the conversation. I gave a brief outline of the events of the past six weeks but no doubt with many gaps. It was 1.00 a.m. before we got to bed so it had been a nineteen-hour day.

I had to get up pretty early again the next day and present myself at the Petroships office at 9.00 a.m. to give a reasonably detailed account of the events from my departure from Singapore through to our release from China—not only for Petroships, but for a lawyer from their insurers. Again, how detailed and coherent this was I can't recall because I was still profoundly tired, physically and mentally, and my brain felt like scrambled eggs. Outside of a one-hour break, this session went on until mid-afternoon when I called a halt. We were due to fly out of Singapore to Brisbane at 7.40 p.m. on Qantas flight QF 52 and there was no way I was going to miss that flight.

There were no hitches at the airport this time and, as we were taxiing to the take-off point, one of the cabin staff advised us that once we were airborne we'd be upgraded to first class. I remember very little about that flight except that Denise enjoyed the food and the experience of flying first class.

'You know, Ken, I could get used to this,' she said.

I gently reminded her that it took for me to be nearly killed for us to get this red carpet treatment. There's a funny side to everything.

At Brisbane airport we were met by a woman from DFAT and two members of the Customs Service. Again, we handed in our baggage tags and passports and bypassed the usual procedures to be taken on another mystery tour of the airport, slipping from arrivals to departure to avoid the press if they happened to be lying in wait. And so I met our daughters with a little privacy and it hit me when we were all together just how rich I was in the things that matter.

It was all very slickly done. We were in our car and on the road with no one in the press having any idea that I was back in the country. And that remained true for a week or so. It was very quiet on the road back to the Gold Coast and I enjoyed the drive and the freedom and the familiarity of the sights and sounds and smells.

We didn't take the usual route home. Instead, I asked Linda, who was driving, to make a detour that would take us a few minutes longer. I remembered the pledge I'd taken when I was taped to the pilot's chair, thinking that any moment soon could be my last. Linda parked outside our local Presbyterian church and I asked Denise, Linda and Wendy to wait a few minutes. I knew a door to the church was always left open and so at 6.30 a.m. on 31 May, 45 days after the hijacking, I kept my part of the deal and had another quiet conversation with God. I simply said, 'Thank you.'

Epilogue

A conspiracy and corruption

After spending two days at home resting, I then set
about catching up with all the print media coverage
that had been published since I and the *Petro Ranger*
had been reported missing. Linda had kept the clippings in several scrapbooks, all carefully dated and
identified. For the first time I was able to discover how
much information had been withheld from me by
Petroships and the Chinese authorities, and how much
misinformation and untruth had been apparently fed
by the company to the media. To date Petroships has
not explained why this was done.

During my four weeks in China I realised that all
was not what it seemed, especially when Mr Tan was
bluntly accused by the Marine Police of being a party
to the piracy operation. After that, my suspicions grew,
but it was not until I was at home and able to view
documents that gave a broad view of the whole event
that I formed the belief that the Chinese could perhaps
be forgiven for jumping to such a conclusion.

Less than two weeks after getting home, I was flown
to Canberra for a so-called debriefing, first by DFAT
and then by the Australian Federal Police and numerous other civilian and military intelligence bodies. The

DFAT meeting lasted only an hour, which was scarcely long enough to scratch the surface. My memory of these meetings is somewhat vague, not only because I was still suffering after-effects of what I'd been through but because the experience of having questions fired at me by a lot of people I didn't know bore an eerie similarity to what had happened in China. I had an instinctive distrust of the questioners and I doubt that they got much detailed or useful information out of me. I believed that I returned to normal soon after coming home but later realised that this was not the case. It took almost six months before I was able to recall, coherently, what had happened. Even now, I have an aversion to crowds and insist on standing at the back of elevators, making sure no one is behind me. Whether sitting in an office, a restaurant or the comfort of my own home, I always sit with my back to the wall and in a position where I have an unobstructed view of all the doorways.

As I see things now, my lack of cooperation may have turned out to be a good thing. I now believe that the whole point of the Canberra exercise was to find out exactly how much I knew because the Australian government was already positioning itself to take the safest diplomatic approach. Relations with China, Malaysia and Singapore were the first priority and DFAT wanted to make sure there was no information floating about that could create a public backlash.

What follows is a list of questions raised by the activities of Petroships during the search for the ship and never answered, and an analysis of the implications of events in China.

1 *Why was the initial twelve-hour delay in Singapore never investigated?*

2 Why did Petroships continually claim that they didn't own the *Petro Ranger* when clearly they did? (See Appendix D.)

3 Why did Petroships not alert all regional governments and authorities on 18 April when they did not receive the noon position report on that date as was legally required in the charter party agreement and also by the company's own regulations? As an Australian Maritime Safety Officer said, the incident 'should have triggered some reaction. Petroships should have raised the alarm.' In this connection, why did Mr Tan 'refuse', as reported in the press, 'to comment on why no alarm was raised or any attempt made to contact the ship when it failed to report in and arrive on Saturday'?

4 The alleged telex, supposedly sent by the ship on 17 April, has never been sighted by me even though Petroships agreed on camera during the filming of a *60 Minutes* segment to supply a photocopy of it. Both the radio operator and myself were tied up and the pirates could not use the communications equipment, therefore who could have sent such a telex?

5 Why did the company claim that the ship's telephones were dead from 17 April when in fact they were not taken out of action until the 19th?

6 Why was my wife not advised that I was missing until 2.45 p.m. on 20 April and why, after she had been so advised, did the company refuse to accept telephone calls from her for the next 21 hours?

7 Why was the assistance of the Singapore Government not sought immediately the ship was deemed to be missing?

8 Why did Petroships not advise the Australian High Commission in Singapore that I was missing and request its assistance until 22 April and only did so on my wife's insistence?

9 Why was the false report about anonymous satellite telephone calls issued?

10 Why was the assistance of the Royal Malaysian Air Force not requested until 24 April?

11 Given that Singapore purports to be a modern, sophisticated state, how could it be that the best it could offer by way of help was to convey Petroships' clairvoyant's report?

12 What were the Singapore authorities' motives in stressing that the *Petro Ranger* was registered in Malaysia and was trading under the Malaysian flag? Why was Singapore so concerned to distance itself from Petroships?

13 These questions all point in the direction of a larger one—did Petroships *want* the *Petro Ranger* to be found?

Sadly, during the early months at home, I held to the belief that an official enquiry would be made into the hijacking by either Malaysia or Singapore but, to date, the only enquiry that has been conducted into the affair has been by China.

The documents issued by the regional office in Manila of the Honduras International Naval Surveying Inspection Bureau in respect of the next ship targeted by the pirates seemed to me to be the starting point for a wide-ranging investigation. The same bureau, incidentally, had issued the documents for my ship under the name MT *Wilby*. Interpol and the various law enforcement bodies in the countries mentioned in these documents could have acted in concert. This was never done.

Australian officials, in possession of these documents, should have brought pressure to bear on these countries to act. On the very night the *Petro Ranger* was hijacked, a pirate attack was made on a large

EPILOGUE

Australian tanker carrying gas from the North-West Shelf field off Western Australia to Japan. The ecological disaster that could have occurred if this attack had succeeded or gone seriously wrong (if, say, heavy weapons had been used or the pirates had mismanaged the tanker's equipment) could have been immense. This attack, which *may* have been merely a diversionary move by the pirates to direct attention away from the *Petro Ranger*, has never been reported, but it shows that no country's shipping is immune from pirate attack.[27]

The only investigation Malaysia made into the piracy was to have the Royal Malaysian Police relay to me in July 1998, through the Australian Federal Police liaison officer at the High Commission in Kuala Lumpur, a set of questions:

1 Could I confirm that I was the Captain of the ship during the incident?

2 Who was the owner of the ship's cargo?

3 What was the ship's destination?

4 What cargo was the ship carrying and what was the amount or weight?

5 Give details of the crew.

6 What was the location of the ship and the time of the attack?

7 Where was the ship taken after the hijacking?

8 Could I identify the pirates if I saw them again and what languages did they speak?

9 Were the hijackers armed?

10 Did any of the crew collaborate with the hijackers?

These were hardly very probing questions and were asked two months after my release from China. It seems fair to conclude that the Malaysian police were only going through the motions.

As for the Chinese, they did not prosecute the pirates and deported them to their countries of origin. A claim made in the press that Malaysia had applied for the extradition of the pirates was false. *The Chinese informed the Australian Consul General's office in Guangzhou on 22 July 1998, that China's wish was to hand the pirates over to be prosecuted in Malaysia, Indonesia or an international authority.*[28] This offer was never responded to. The Chinese claim that they did not have the evidence to prosecute for piracy was true *because the relevant evidence had been handed over to Petroships.* On 28 May, when documentation was exchanged between Petroships and the PSB, included was a letter of undertaking to the PSB and the Marine Police that Petroships would agree to sign for the MT *Wilby* (or *Petro Ranger*). This wording was dictated by the PSB, which insisted that the ship still be called the *Wilby.* What this meant was that when I signed for the ship's documentation to be returned to the company the false documents for the MT *Wilby* were given to Petroships as well as the official documents for the *Petro Ranger*. A document in the exchange stating that Enerfrate appointed Petroships as managers of the *Petro Ranger* dated 26 May 1996 was clearly a forgery as the ship did not go under Malaysian registration until September of that year. The company seemed to have been muddying the waters as much as it could. Also Petroships always owned the *Petro Ranger*, so how could Enerfrate appoint the company as 'managers'? If anything, it should have been the other way around. These documents also raise the question of why the Public Notary in Singapore stamped and signed them on 26 May, two days before the ship's release.

The Chinese were thus left in possession of all the money taken from the pirates' sale of part of the cargo and the rest of the cargo, all to be used as 'evidence'. But with the critical documentary evidence regarding

Petroships Pte Ltd

450 Alexandra Road
#25-04 PSA Building
Singapore 119963

Telephone : 273 1122
Telex : RS 24176
Fax : 273 2200

Letter of Undertaking

To: Hainan Province Public Security Bureau
. Hainan Province Marine Police No.1 Branch Station

In view of the continuing investigation by your Bureau (Station) into suspected smuggling involving MV "Wilby" (or MV "Petro Ranger") and 21-crew members employed by our company and the claim by our company and the 21 crew members of hijack at sea, we, Petroships Pte Ltd, residing at 460 Alexandra Road #25-04 PSA Building Singapore 119963, being managers of the "Petro Ranger", hereby apply to your Bureau (Station) for bail of the "Wilby" (or the "Petro Ranger") and the 21 crew members employed by us (crew list attached). Should further investigation be required by your Bureau (Station), we undertake to cooperate with your Bureau (Station) in the investigation of the "Wilby" (or the "Petro Ranger") and to make the 21 crew members available promptly for investigation by your Bureau (Station) provided they are in our employ.

After bail is granted by your Bureau (Station), we shall be responsible for the safety of the 21 crew members.

Tan Cheng Mong
Executive Director

For and on behalf of
Petroships Pte Ltd

26 May 1998

7. Letter of Undertaking dated 26 May 1998 in which Petroships agrees to sign bail for the 'MV "Wilby"'

Enerfrate Sdn Bhd

(Co. No. 388607-H)

P.O. Box 125
Port Dickson 71007

Tel : 06-647 9202
Fax : 06-647 9200

27 May 1996

Petroships Pte Ltd
460 Alexandra Road
#25-04 PSA Building
Singapore 119963

Dear Sirs

APPOINTMENT AS MANAGER OF ENERFRATE VESSELS

We are pleased to appoint Petroships Pte Ltd (Petroships) as the manager of the vessel "Petro Ranger", Official No. 327292, that is presently owned by Enerfrate Sdn Bhd.

The appointment shall be effective from 27 May 1996 and shall apply to other vessels that may be owned by Enerfrate Sdn Bhd in the future.

As the manager of the vessel, Petroships shall be responsible for operation of the vessel and shall also take over all the duties and responsibility imposed by the International Safety Management (ISM) Code.

Yours faithfully
ENERFRATE SDN BHD

Kenneth Kee
Director

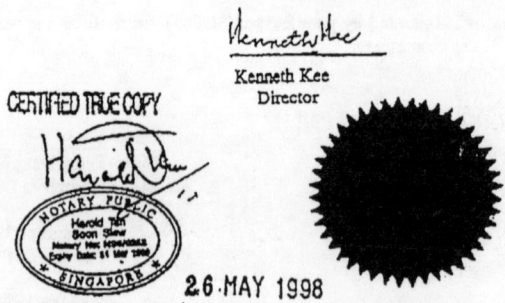

CERTIFIED TRUE COPY

Harold Tan
Boon Siew
Notary Mac Separated
Expiry Date: 11 May 1998

26 MAY 1998

1st Floor, Wisma MCA, 463 Jalan Bahru, 71000 Port Dickson, Malaysia

8. A Letter of Appointment dated 27 May 1996 from Enerfrate, appointing Petroships as the *manager* of the *Petro Ranger*. Note that the Public Notary's stamp is dated 26 May.

EPILOGUE

460 Alexandra Road
#25-04 PSA Building
Singapore 119963

Telephone : 273 1122
Telex : RS 24176
Fax : 273 2200

28 May 1996

Enerfrate Sdn Bhd
1ˢᵗ floor, Wisma MCA
483, Jalan Bahru
71000, Port Dickson
Malaysia

Dear Sirs

APPOINTMENT AS MANAGER OF ENERFRATE VESSEL

Many thanks for your letter dated 27 May 1997 appointing Petroships Pte Ltd as the manager of "Petro Ranger", Official No. 327292, a Malaysian registered vessel owned by your Company.

As the manager of the vessel, we shall be responsible for the operation of the vessel as well as undertake all the duties and responsibilities imposed by the International Safety management (ISM) code.

Yours faithfully
PETROSHIPS PTE LTD

Tan Cheng Meng
Executive Director

CERTIFIED TRUE COPY

9. Letter dated 28 May 1996 from Petroships to Enerfrate, confirming Petroships' appointment as the manager of the *Petro Ranger*.

143

the piracy in possession of the company and no prosecution possible, the ultimate fate of this 'evidence'
can only be speculated about. Also no investigation
of the highly likely conspiracy between the PSB and
the pirates could be held. Which is not to say that the
Chinese didn't do their own house-cleaning. Judging
from the attitude of the Commissar and the Marine
Police, I suspect that the corrupt PSB officers and
the Chinese members of the syndicate have been
summarily dealt with.

Presumably, the Chinese were happy with the outcome: they had the money and the fuel and could
depict themselves as having behaved correctly. Likewise, Malaysia, Indonesia and Singapore, with much
to lose in terms of the involvement of their nationals
and enterprises in large-scale crime if a searching
enquiry were held, were in the clear. It seems likely
that those four governments came to a mutually beneficial, if somewhat unorthodox, arrangement.

Australia, which is to say DFAT, has, I believe, more
knowledge of circumstances involving Malaysia and
Singapore and what took place in China regarding both
the piracy and the ultimate release of the ship. But I
believe that the matter has been treated in a *diplomatic*
fashion, that is with the classification of certain documents and the withholding of others, all in the interest
of relations with Singapore and Malaysia, rather than
in a way designed to get to the truth. I believe I was
lied to. It was only by chance that documents proving
that Australia knew of China's intentions regarding the
pirates as early as 22 July 1998 came into my hands.
But nothing was done. I cannot compliment and thank
the consular section of DFAT enough for the help given
me during my four weeks in China, especially Zena
Armstrong, Consul General in Guangzhou and most of
all the Vice-Consul Graham Pearce and Daisy Pearce.
But other sections of DFAT fell far short of them in
integrity and competence.

EPILOGUE

After their arrival in Singapore, I believe that some of the officers and crew left the sea. Others presumably joined other companies and other ships. I have not kept in touch with any crew members apart from Saini Ungie, who played a valiant role in my escape and will be a friend for life.

I believe the hijacking of the *Petro Ranger* will stay in all our minds for the rest of our lives. I learned a lot, especially about myself, from the experience.

Recently, an Indian airliner was hijacked and, sadly, one passenger was killed. He died because he didn't do as he was told, namely, to bow his head and not look at the faces of the hijackers. As I learned myself, the initial stages of a hijacking—until the victims and their surroundings have been secured—are the most dangerous as the terrorists or, in my case, pirates are agitated and scared. This was why and when the unfortunate airline passenger was killed—for not doing as he was told. As I'm not writing a handbook for hijackers, I won't elaborate on this topic.

The last question is what happened to the pirates. The men who hijacked the *Petro Ranger* were released by the Chinese and sent to Indonesia in mid-October. Not a long time in custody for a crime such as theirs, although I'm sure it was 'hard time'. Shortly afterwards a Singaporean citizen named Chen Cheng Kait (aka 'Mr Wong'), who was the Singaporean member of the pirate syndicate, was arrested by the Indonesian navy. He was sentenced to six years' jail for various offences.

I have no idea what happened to Herman and his men. My suspicion is that they were forced by the Indonesian authorities to reveal all they knew and this led to the arrest of 'Mr Wong'. I doubt that they are still alive. Until one of the governments in the area holds a thorough investigation into this affair, the true extent of the pirate operation will never be known and its continued existence will not be threatened. Already, and sadly, other attacks have occurred and the pirates have taken care to leave no witnesses. And until such an enquiry proves otherwise, I will live with the disturbing suspicion that someone or some persons with some connection to Petroships were a part of the pirate conspiracy.

Insurance is at the heart of the real cost of piracy and hijacking of shipping. Human life, other than for the nations of Australia, New Zealand, Europe, Japan, Canada and the United States is, in reality, classed as expendable.

Hijacking of ships, politics and corruption, all veiled in lies and secrecy, are a huge cost to the insurers of the ships involved. The cost to insurers is estimated to be between $US200 and $US400 million annually. Due to the confidentiality surrounding Lloyds and other insurers, an exact figure is never made available.

It is not a loss that would bring Lloyds to its knees, but it contributes to the high losses some syndicates of Lloyds incur each year, reaching a point where Lloyds' syndicates are seriously considering withdrawing from this area of business in certain South-East Asian areas and from various shipping companies operating in this region. An example of what insurers face and have to deal with can be seen in my case. On 5 May 1998, Mr Li Xuiling of the Hainan Foreign Affairs news office reported that the twelve alleged *Petro Ranger* pirates were in custody in Haikou. This was true. He further stated that the ship's crew were not in custody and were regarded as free.

Mr Li reported that most of the cargo was still on the ship. Two of Petroships' representatives in Haikou had been refused permission by the Chinese authorities to board and inspect the ship and the balance of cargo remaining aboard.

These latest revelations only added to puzzling questions surrounding the *Petro Ranger* mystery. Petroships had and still have refused to say why it took several days to alert maritime authorities that its tanker was missing.

China has not explained why it did not report locating the ship for three days, despite an international alert on its disappearance. The press release from Mr Li and the above comments were widely reported in the Australian press of 5 May 1998 and demonstrate the problems insurers face when trying to gain true pictures of claims made upon them.

Police forces in the region want nothing to do with the problem. Their usual answer to critics is that they have no authority in international waters. The International Maritime Bureau estimates that only 2 per cent of piracy occurs in international waters!

If a ship owner has a ship hijacked and if he is lucky enough to locate it, he may find it cheaper to pay rival pirates to seize it back, rather than trying to legally regain the ship. Two or three years ago, a ship called the *Erria Inge* was hijacked but, after being sighted in international waters, it was suggested to the owners by a Singapore official that they pay for its re-hijacking. The going rate was $500 000 to have your ship grabbed and sailed to the port of your choice. This could also involve the crew being thrown overboard—a popular way of keeping witnesses quiet and cutting down on food consumption.

Another contributing factor to not knowing fully the extent of the cost of piracy is, and I quote the International Maritime Bureau's own words here, 'that many shipowners do not report attacks—or make late reports—to avoid delays and additional costs. Moreover, reporting an attack can cause insurance problems and do commercial damage to a company. The real figure for attacks is estimated to be about double the official figure'.

Again, I must stress the ease with which ships' registration papers can be bought from a 'flag of convenience' country's Embassy and Consulates, by simply supplying a ship's description. This is corroborated by many members of the international shipping community.

Below are tabulated figures supplied by the International Maritime Bureau for 1998 which I only discovered existed after leaving China and starting my own investigation into piracy.

In the Far East and South-East Asia in the Year 1998
66　crew members were killed
11　crew members were injured
29　crew members were assaulted
114　crew members were taken hostage
12　ships were hijacked in this same area in 1998.

Out of a total of 15 ships hijacked in 1998, 12 hijackings occurred in the Far East and South-East Asia. Worldwide, in 1998, a further 138 ships were attacked and boarded.

Other documented examples of piracy and hijacking in South-East Asia in 1998 are:

1. China: The 2660 ton, Panamanian flag cargo ship *Tenyu*, reported missing on 13 October with a cargo of alumina ingots worth $1.9 million, was located on 21 December in the Chinese port of Zhanjiang, South China. (It was reported as Zhangjiajang in North China, but thought to be as stated above, as action was taken by Guangzhou Maritime Court.) The ship had been renamed *Sanei 1*, although the actual vessel of that name was confirmed as being in service between Japanese ports. Chinese authorities are reported to have detained the crew of sixteen Indonesians working aboard the ship. There is no report on the whereabouts of the thirteen Chinese and two South Koreans who formed the original crew. *The ship reportedly currently contains a cargo of palm oil worth an estimated $2.2 million, believed stolen in a separate mid-year piracy incident* (but for which the Office of Naval Intelligence, or ONI, holds no further data) *or potentially stolen from a legitimate shipper by use of* Sanei 1 *as a phantom vessel.* The renaming of the ship and its apparent ability to trade undetected since October, plus the presence of a cargo believed stolen even earlier leads to the conclusion that the hijack was the work of a highly organised gang. China, which is already under intense criticism for the 15 October release without trial of the Indonesians suspected in the 17 April hijacking of the Malaysian tanker *Petro Ranger* will be watched closely in its handling of this latest incident. *Tenyu* formerly reported under South China Sea–Strait of Malacca heading. (*Office of Naval Intelligence*)

As related, I suspect the cargo of palm oil and the vessel referred to above relate to the *Surin* papers which were left behind by the pirates of the *Petro Ranger*, which papers I subsequently found and forwarded with a covering letter to the Australian Department of Foreign Affairs and Trade in late May 1998.

2. *China:* Chinese police announced 5 March that they had arrested 20 more persons in the *Cheung Son* hijack. They simultaneously announced that the seizure off Hong Kong had been accomplished by the gang posing as Chinese customs officials. Public Security Bureau (China) announced 12 January that it had arrested members of a piracy gang in the hijack of the 10 373 ton Panamanian flag *Cheung Son* and murder of its 23 Chinese crew. The arrested men reported admit to having seized the ship for a payment of $US11 000 each and were reportedly found with photographs of a celebration party aboard. Earlier in the week Chinese authorities had identified three of six bodies caught in fishermen's nets off Shantou, China, as being those

of *Cheung Son* crew members. *The bodies had reportedly been bound, gagged and weighted.* Theft of a ship with a cargo of furnace slag worth only $US65 000 leads industry analysts to believe the ship was either taken in error or was seized for use as a phantom vessel. Phantom vessels are used to secure legitimate cargo which is then stolen from its owner and diverted for black market sale (see *Tenyu* report above). Chinese authorities, which have been under criticism since the release without trial of the Indonesians found in control of the tanker *Petro Ranger* in mid-October, will now be watched closely in their handling of the Chinese perpetrators of the *Cheung Son* incident and the Indonesians arrested aboard *Tenyu*, whose crew must also be presumed to have died.

3. South China Sea: The International Maritime Bureau (IMB) has announced a reward of up to $US50 000 for information leading to the location and recovery of ship and/or cargo in the case of the 3113-ton cargo ship *Hong Peng*. *Hong Peng* disappeared after departing Hong Kong 26 December for Taizhong, Taiwan with a cargo of clay and a crew of 20. In view of the murder of the crew of *Cheung Son* and apparent hijack of the ship with a low value cargo of furnace slag, this disappearance of a ship with a similarly low value cargo raises fears that yet another crew may have been murdered and another ship taken for use as a phantom vessel.

4. China–South Korea: South Korean authorities in Inchon arrested three Koreans on 20 February on charges of acquiring a cargo stolen from the hijacked *Tenyu*. One of the three has reportedly admitted purchasing the vessel and its cargo from two Chinese-Indonesians and selling them to a Chinese company in October 1998. (*Office of Naval Intelligence*)

By official estimates smuggling, which includes piracy, costs China up to $US12 billion a year, more than 1 per cent of gross domestic product (GDP) and equivalent to 6.5 per cent of total exports for 1997. Add the loss of tax revenues and the financial losses to domestic producers and it could add up to 3 or 4 per cent of GDP, according to Salomon Brothers in Hong Kong. Early in 1998, President Jiang Zenin ordered the People's Liberation Army to get out of all illegal businesses it had set up and appointed a special police force to root out government employees who engage in, or turn a blind eye to, corruption and piracy.

Such corruption was a reality that the Chinese government knew, but did not admit, infiltrated as the illicit trade was by its armed forces, so the government had resolved to end the link between the black market and its employees.

Nowhere is the impact of smuggling more pervasive than in commodities. Industries have come to rely on smuggled copper, aluminium, cotton, chemicals and crude oil. Massive losses by the state oil giant China National Petroleum Corp. in the first four months of 1998 ($US325 million) alarmed the government.

High domestic Chinese oil prices have led to a hijack-to-order industry in the South China Sea. According to the International Maritime Bureau, oil tankers are systematically pirated and taken into Chinese ports, where false documents are routinely accepted by Customs authorities.

'Nowhere else in the world do you have these crimes, where ships are taken over by pirates with full sets of documents for both the vessel registration and the cargo,' an International Maritime Bureau director said.

Recent events demonstrate that Jiang Zenin's new tough policies on piracy and corruption are taking effect. In January 2000, China executed 13 pirates who, in December 1999, had been convicted of murdering 23 sailors in the country's worst single hijacking in 50 years, that of the *Cheung Son* (see page 148). Of the 38 pirates in the gang, 19 were sentenced to terms between 10 months and life, while six were acquitted due to their testimony against their erstwhile accomplices. Although the Chinese police claimed that the leader of the pirates was an Indonesian named Sonny Wei, Wei maintained that the order to kill the crew of the *Cheung Son* came from a Shanwei businessman, who took no actual part in the hijacking. Chinese police have confirmed that they are holding someone in connection with the hijacking. The international community waits to see whether China will maintain her new hardline approach to piracy.

At the time of going to press, there are unconfirmed reports that a Japanese-registered vessel, with an international crew, will shortly be patrolling the South China Sea on a regular basis. This is obviously an encouraging advance in the international war against piracy.

Endnotes

1 This twelve-hour delay is one of the critical points in the story of the *Petro Ranger*. See endnote 4.
2 See Appendix D for information on the International Maritime Bureau and a summary of its findings about three pirate attacks, including that on the *Petro Ranger*.
3 The pretext was that they would be signing on a ship anchored off the coast of Malaysia which had been sold for scrap to Japan and that they would then be flown back to Singapore. They were taken to Johore Baru to await a small boat to take them out to the ship. Once on the boat they discovered what was really happening. They were innocent victims of circumstance, in the wrong place at the wrong time.
4 *This points up the importance of the delay in Singapore. Had the ship left on schedule it would have been at the hijack point at half past one in the afternoon of the 16th. Clear daylight!* Pirates can only operate at night. I suspect that Shell employees were bribed to contrive the delay but, like many other aspects of the case, this was never investigated.
5 Global Positioning System—a satellite receiver that

continuously gives the vessel's position, speed and other navigational information.

6   We also had audio tapes, mostly of popular music. At one point someone played a tape of Indian music and I was reminded of the Indian music that had been played on the bridge courtesy of that officer who'd left his post. I practically walked over a couple of bodies and shouted, 'Get that bloody thing off.' I never want to hear Indian music again as long as I live.

7   I have the greatest admiration for the members of the Australian Defence Forces who participated in this operation. An organised search was accomplished within eighteen hours of my wife's notification by Petroships, very quick work and all done in an unofficial capacity. By contrast, Petroships had still not yet advised all government authorities and did not do so until long after the RAAF's action.

8   The Marine or Water Police is a unit within the PLA. Its members are soldiers rather than policemen, similar to the American coast guard or the military police in western armies.

9   I will never forget the name of the officer in charge at this time, Lieutenant Pei An Li.

10   Oddly, the barred door was covered with a rather beautiful piece of Chinese ornamentation.

11   What neither Denise nor Petroships knew was that the Haikou fax number they'd been given was the *Commissar's* number and all faxes to me were vetted first by him. None were withheld from me.

12   In fact this was untrue. The weather, apart from some rain, was good throughout my time in China. It was simply the case that it suited the Chinese to delay my meeting with the consular people until after the crew were released back to the ship. Mr Tan, Captain Jerries and Mr Li had no difficulty in getting to Hainan.

13 This falsehood appeared, for example, in the Brisbane *Courier Mail*, 5 May 1998, under a headline which was one of the silliest—'Pirates took my tanker: captain.'

14 The telephones in several places on the ship were not disabled by the pirates until 19 April, one day after we were due to arrive in Ho Chi Minh City. On that day the pirate who was supposed to be able to use the communications equipment but couldn't, asked my radio operator why these telephones were ringing. The radio operator explained that they were the satellite telephones connected to Singapore. The pirates pulled them from the wall. The significance of this is that Petroships' claim to have attempted to telephone the ship on the 17th and 18th was false. No attempt was made until the 19th.

15 This was the only physical ill treatment by the Chinese that I saw but I know that the leader had been savagely kicked some time before. Saini, the Malaysian seaman who spoke some Mandarin, had been used as an interpreter when the Chinese interrogated the leader. He said he saw them kicking him as he was on the cement floor of the cell and shouting at him, 'Why should we believe you? You tell us different things each time.'

16 *Courier Mail*, 6/5/98; *Gold Coast Bulletin*, 8/5/98; *Courier Mail*, 8/5/98; *Adelaide Advertiser*, 8/5/98; *South Coast Morning Post*, 8/5/98; *Sydney Daily Telegraph*, 9/5/98. A curious feature of Bolt's reports is the inaccuracy of the dates. In his *Adelaide Advertiser* account he states that he visited the *Petro Ranger* on Monday and Tuesday; in the *Daily Telegraph* the days are given as Tuesday and Wednesday, but the dates of his visits cannot be other than Thursday 7 May and Friday 8 May. Andrew Bolt, who wrote reams about me in China, has never contacted me since.

17 *Sun-Herald*, 10/5/98.

18 Cigarettes and tobacco are bought by the shipowners at duty free rates and delivered to the vessel in bonded packages. The Captain then sells them to the crew at the duty free price, a considerable reduction. The cost is subsequently deducted from their wages.

19 Our plan *had* been to have dinner with family and friends and then a short holiday, probably in New Zealand.

20 I'm not sure when, or even if, consuls from the Philippines, Bangladesh and Indonesia arrived to help their nationals. The Ghanaian Consul arrived only a few days before the ship left.

21 Sadly, this never happened and, while I believe that the consular section of DFAT is the best in the world, I don't hold the same opinion of other sections of the department. See below for analysis and discussion that questions the truthfulness and competence of elements within DFAT.

22 I next heard of Mr Wong in November 1998 when he was arrested by the Indonesian navy. A Singaporean, he was the piracy syndicate's representative in Singapore and West Malaysia, that is, Kuala Lumpur and Johore Baru. As such, he was primarily responsible for planning and organising the hijacking of the *Petro Ranger*.

23 Apparently others had made the same comparison. A report in *The Australian* of 7/5/98 was headed 'Skipper stranded in Chinese Wild West'.

24 That is, with the exception of Denise's and my brief excursion to the markets and, more importantly, my taking of the pirates' ship-hijacking documents which I still had in my possession.

25 Much later, after my return to Australia, I discovered why the ship had never been taken alongside a wharf. If it had, the line of demarcation in authority between the Marine Police and the

PSB would have been crossed and the Marine Police would have ceased to have any input and the PSB would have been the sole investigating agency. Fortunately, the Commissar apparently had the power to prevent this or things could have turned out very differently.

26 The notarised documents required by the PSB are discussed in the Epilogue.

27 With a better trained crew and officers, the tanker managed to evade the pirates.

28 Copies of documents to this effect were obtained by the Consul General's office, Guangzhou on 2 June 1998, five days after the ship was released.

Appendix A

This is a reproduction of the covering letter I wrote before being released from China, in which I explained the significance of the documents I had found on the *Petro Ranger*. Facsimiles of the actual documents themselves can be found in Appendices B and C.

To Whom It May Concern

19th May 1998

The enclosed documents were found by me after the China Marine Police had searched my ship, and [I] decided they should be hidden until I could get them to Australian Authorities.

This is not an account of my piracy experience (that is another tale) but pieces of documented evidence how numerous nations have, and still are, involved in this filthy business of piracy/murder on the organisational side of these deeds. I will set out these countries individually and their involvement. Also this is proof of not only was my ship targeted to be pirated on the night 16/17 April but a second ship to be renamed MT Surin was also targeted and these false documents for this vessel are the ones I found. Please note the false ship's papers were issued on the 16th March, one month before the ships were to be taken, indicating these operations are planned well in advance of the actual act. To find out the actual name of the MT Surin you will have to check back on all tankers sailing with a cargo of Palm Oil from Indonesia or Malaysia around 15/16 April as indicated on the false Bills of Lading. In short this is selective Piracy for valuable cargoes, i.e. Piracy on order.

Republic of Honduras.
This country is supplying the blank false ships' documents and official papers.

Philippines.
This nation is guilty of issuing the false documents through a CAPTAIN RAUL PINEDAT, Surveyor to the Honduras Naval Inspection Bureau and whose actual signature appears on the following documents:

Cargo Ship Safety Construction Certificate
International Oil Pollution Prevention Certificate
International Load Liner Certificate
Cargo Ship Safety Equipment Certificate
International Tonnage Certificate
Cargo Ship Radio Telegraphy Certificate

Please note these certificates were issued on the 16th March *1998.*

On the Certificate of Registry you will note it was also issued on the 16th March and signed by the C in C Naval Forces Honduras and states the owners as
Sea King Shipping Co. S. De. R.L.
Belgium
and
Oswaldo Da Costa as the representative also Fukae Zosen Horoshima is mentioned.
So you can see after the ships are pirated, their cargoes are sold illegally then, the Registry of the ship is changed in this case to Honduras and then sold on paper to the Sea King Shipping Co in Belgium and then either used for legal trading or sold on the open market as a going concern. So you can see it is a very lucrative business indeed involving millions and millions of U.S. dollars.

Indonesia:
    You will see from the blank Port Clearance Certif'e enclosed it only has the official stamp and the Selaku Harbour Masters signature on it, so allowing the pirates to fill in any ships details and so making it a legal document allowing entry into any port in the world. I believe one of the people heading this organisation is from Jakarta.

Taiwan:
    You can see from the false Bills of Lading the consignee is
        First Enterprise Co Ltd.
        9F No 391 Shin Yi Rd Sec 4
        Taipei Taiwan
        R.O.C.

Also this company's name is nominated on the enclosed invoice and the cargo supposedly transported to
    Kaohsiung Port Taiwan.

Malaysia:
    All false Bills of Lading were issued in Malaya nominating the Shipper as
        T.G.E. Enterprise
        32 Jalan Nagasari 16
        Segamat Johor Malaysia

and
    the consignee as the aforeseaid Co. in Taiwan.
    Note the Bills of Lading are stamped 15th April and my ship sailed on 16th April. Also the Paul Shipping Co. is named on these documents.
The pirates also departed from Malaya when setting out to hijack my ship.

Finally I believe Malaya is the principle [sic] country where all planning and recruitment of pirates takes place and where the decisions are made as to which ships to capture. Although I cannot prove it, it may be with the assistance of certain government bodies . . . Singapore False passports for pirates and recruitment of personnel are from this nation.

It should be noted it took an unusually long time to load my cargo in Singapore and I believe this was done so that my departure from Singapore would work in with the pirates pre planned rendezvous time with my ship. Plus I have often wondered why the Harbour Pilot (Singapore) sarcastically wished me a 'safe' voyage rather than the usual 'Have a good trip Captain'. The pirates were also fully aware of the exact time the Harbour Pilot departed from my ship so I kindly requested both Singapore Harbour's Loading Masters and the Harbour Pilot be investigated.

Finally it was brought to my attention by the Pirate Capt. that he had my name, address, phone number and immediate family details and could have any of my family killed at any time if he so wanted.
Question:

How did he acquire these details, suggest Petroships staff also be fully investigated. The Pirate Capt. also boasted the heads of his organisation resided in Malaysia, Singapore, Indonesia, Hong Kong and China.

On my release from China I will be available to assist you in any way I can to rid this evil act of piracy on the high seas.

I kindly request the appropriate trusted personnel in the Singapore Security Forces also be given these details and would they supply protection to both my wife and myself on your upcoming visit to Singapore on my release from here as there are numerous insurance documents etc I have to deal with in relation to the stolen cargo etc.

Please be careful who you discuss all of this with on the Malaysian side of things as I have no trust in them—only Singapore.

In conclusion I hope this and the enclosed documents may be of help to you.

Yours faithfully

CAPTAIN KEN BLYTH

Appendix B

PETRO-PIRATES

REPUBLICA DE HONDURAS
REPUBLIC OF HONDURAS

CERTIFICADO INTERNACIONAL DE ARQUEO (1969)
INTERNATIONAL TONNAGE CERTIFICATE (1969)

Expedido en virtud de las disposiciones del Convenio Internacional sobre Arqueo de Buques, 1969, en nombre del Gobierno de la República de Honduras
Issued under the provisions of the International Convention on Tonnage Measurement of Ships, 1969, under the authority of the Government of the Republic of Honduras

Certificate No 3362142

Nombre del Buque Name of Ship	Señal Distintiva Distinctive Number or Letters	Puerto de Matricula Port of Registry	Fecha Date
M.T. SURIN	HQXT 10	SAN LORENZO	1985

Fecha en la que se puso quilla o en el que el Buque estaba en un estado equivalente de adelanto de su construcción (Artículos 2(6)) ó fecha en la que el buque sufrió transformaciones o modificaciones importantes (Artículo 3(2)(b)), según proceda.
* Date on which the keel was laid or the ship was at a similar stage of construction (Article 2(6)), or date on which the ship underwent alterations or modifications of a major character (Article 3(2) (b)), as appropriate.

DIMENSIONES PRINCIPALES
MAIN DIMENSION

Eslora (Artículo 2(8)) Length (Article 2(8))	Manga (Regla 2(3)) Breadth (Regulation 2(3))	Puntal de trazado hasta la cubierta superior en centro del buque (Regla 2(2)) Moulded Depth amidships to Upper Deck (Regulation 2(2))
97.25 M	16.50 M	5.25 M

LOS ARQUEOS DEL BUQUE SON:
THE TONNAGES OF THE SHIP ARE:

AQUEO BRUTO   3151.61 .... ARQUEO NETO 1365.21
GROSS TONNAGE   NET TONNAGE

Se certifica que los arqueos de este buque han sido determinados de acuerdo con las disposiciones del Convenio Internacional sobre Arqueo de Buques, 1969.
This is the Certify that the tonnages of this ship have been determined in accordance with the provisions of the International Convention of Tonnage Measurement of Ships, 1969.

Expedido en MANILA PHILIPPINES .... el día .... 16 MARCH 1998
Issued at   on the

El infrascrito declara que esta está debidamente autorizado por el Gobierno arriba mencionado para expedir este certificado.
The undersigned declares that he is duly authorized by the said Government to issue this certificate.

CAPT. RUAL PINEDA

....
INSPECTOR DE/SURVEYOR TO
COMPANIA NACIONAL DE REGISTRO E
INSPECCION DE NAVES S. DE R.L.

F NO: 332716

163

PETRO-PIRATES

Certificado de Seguridad Radiotelegráfica para Buque de Carga
Cargo Ship Safety Radiotelegraphy Certificate

REPUBLICA DE HONDURAS

INTERIM Pending issurance of full term certificate

EXPEDIDO EN VIRTUD DE LAS DISPOSICIONES DEL CONVENIO INTERNACIONAL
PARA LA SEGURIDAD DE LA VIDA HUMANA EN EL MAR, 1960
*ISSUED UNDER THE PROVISIONS OF THE INTERNATIONAL CONVENTION
FOR THE SAFETY OF LIFE AT SEA, 1960*

RTG 1500-

Nombre del buque *Name of ship*	Número o letras distintivos *Distinctive Number of letters*	Puerto de matricula *Port of Registry*	Arqueo bruto *Gross Tonnage*	Fecha en que se coloco la quilla (vease NOTA) *Date on which keel was laid (see note below)*
M.T. SURIN	HQXT 10	SAN LORENZO	3151.61MT	1985

El abajo firmante,
I, the undersigned　　CAPT. RUAL PINEDA

Certifica
certify

I.　Que el buque arriba mencionado cumple con lo prescrito en las Reglas anexas al citado Convenio, en lo que respecta a radiotelegrafía y radar, del modo siguiente:
That the above-mentioned ship complies with the provisions of the Regulations annexed to the Convention referred to above as regards Radiotelegraphy:

	Prescripciones de las Reglas *Requirements of Regulations*	Disposiciones y equipos existentes a bordo *Actual provision*
Hora de escucha por operador *Hours of listening by operator*	CONTINUOUS	CONTINUOUS
Numero de operadores *Number of operators*	TO BE FITTED	FITTED
¿Hay autoalarma? *Whether auto alarm fitted*	TO BE FITTED	FITTED
¿Hay instalacion principal? *Whether main installation fitted*	TO BE FITTED	FITTED
¿Hay instalacion de reserva? *Whether reserve installation fitted*	TO BE FITTED	FITTED
¿El transmisor principal y el de reserva, estan electricamente separados o combinados? *Whether main and reserve transmitters electrically separated or combined*	TO BE SEPARATED	SEPARATED
¿Hay radiogoniometro? *Whether direction-finder fitted*	TO BE FITTED *	FITTED

El presente certificado se expide con autoridad conferida por el Gobierno de la Republica de Honduras.
This certificate is issued under the authority of the Republic of Honduras.

Sera valido hasta.　　AUGUST 16, 1998
It will remain in force until

Expedido en　MANILA　　　　el　　16　　de　　MARCH　　de 19. 98
Issued at　　PHILIPPINES　　　*the*　　　　*day of*

El Infrascrito declara que ... izado por el expresado Gobierno para expedir el ...

The undersigned decl... authorised by the said Government to issue t...

INSPECTOR O... HINSIS

CAPT. RUAL PINEDA

NOTA- Bastara con indicar el ano en que la quilla fue colocada o en que la construccion del buque se hallaba en una fase equivalente, salvo por lo que respecta a 1952, 1965 y 1980, casos en los que se debera consignar la fecha completa.

NOTE- It will be sufficient to indicate the year in which the keel was laid or when the ship was at a similar stage of construction except for 1952, 1965 and 1980, in which cases the actual date should be given.

PETRO-PIRATES

Certificado de Seguridad Del Equipo para Buque de Carga
Cargo Ship Safety Equipment Certificate

REPUBLICA DE HONDURAS
REPUBLIC OF HONDURAS

EXPEDIDO EN VIRTUD DE LAS DISPOSICIONES DEL CONVENIO INTERNACIONAL
PARA LA SEGURIDAD DE LA VIDA HUMANA EN EL MAR, 1960
*ISSUED UNDER THE PROVISIONS OF THE INTERNATIONAL CONVENTION
FOR THE SAFETY OF LIFE AT SEA, 1960*

SE 1500-

INTERIM Validity not to exceed five months
Pending issuance of full term certificate

Nombre del buque *Name of ship*	Número o letras distintivos *Distinctive Number of letters*	Puerto de matricula *Port of Registry*	Arqueo bruto *Gross Tonnage*	Fecha en que se coloco la quilla (véase NOTA) *Date on which keel was laid (see note below)*
M.T. SURIN	HQXT 10	SAN LORENZO	3151.61MT	1985

El abajo firmante,
I the undersigned CAPT. RUAL PINEDA

Certifica
certify

I. Que el buque arriba mencionado ha sido objeto de reconocimiento de conformidad con lo dispuesto en el citado Convenio.
That the above-mentioned ship has been duly inspected in accordance with the provisions of the Convention referred to above.

II. Que el reconocimiento ha puesto de manifiesto que los dispositivos de salvamento bastan para un total, que no podrá ser excedido, de
2 personas, dichos dispositivos son:
That the inspection showed that the life-saving appliances provided for a total number of 30 *persons and no more viz.:-*

1 botes salvavidas situados a babor, con capacidad para acomodar a 30 personas;
lifeboats on port side capable of accommodating 30 persons;

2 botes salvavidas situados a estribor, con capacidad para acomodar a persons;
lifeboats on starboard side capable of accommodating 30 persons

2 botes salvavidas a motor (comprendidos en el total de botes salvavidas que se acaba de indicar), incluidos botes salvavidas a motor provistos de instalacion radiotelegrafica y proyector, y botes salvavidas a motor provistos solamente de proyector;
motor lifeboats (included in the total lifeboats shown above), including motor lifeboats fitted with radiotelegraph installation and searchlight, and motor lifeboats fitted with searchlight only;

8 balsas salvavidas para las que se necesitan dispositivos aprobados de arriado con capacidad para acomodar a 20 personas; y
liferafts, for which approved launching devices are required, capable of accommodating 20 persons; and

30 balsas salvavidas para las que no se necesitan dispositivos aprobados de arriado, con capacidad para acomodar a personas;
liferafts, for which approved launching devices are not required, capable of accommodating persons;

20 aros salvavidas;
lifebuoys;

chalecos salvavidas.
lifejackets.

III. Que los botes y las balsas salvavidas van provistos del equipo prescrito en las Reglas anexas al Convenio.
That the lifeboats and liferafts were equipped with the provisions of the Regulations annexed to the Convention.

IV. Que el buque va provisto de aparato lanzacabos y de aparato radioelectrico portatil para embarcacion de supervivencia, de conformidad con lo dispuesto en las Reglas.
That the ship was provided with a line-throwing apparatus and portable radio apparatus for survival craft in accordance with the provisions of the Regulations.

V. Que el reconocimiento ha puesto de manifiesto que el buque cumple con las prescripciones del convenio citado en cuanto a los dispositivos de extincion de incendios y a los pianos de los sistemas de lucha contra incendios, ecosonda y girocompas, y que esta provisto de luces y marcas de navegacion y de una escala de practico, asi como de medios emisores de senales acusticas y de socorro, de conformidad con lo dispuesto en las Reglas y en el vigente Reglamento internacional para prevenir los abordajes en el mar.
That the inspection showed that the ship complied with the requirements of the said Convention as regards fire-extinguishing appliances and fire control plans, echo-sounding device and gyro-compass and was provided with navigation lights and shapes, pilot ladder, and means of making sound signals and distress signals, in accordance with the provisions of the Regulations and the International Regulations for Preventing Collisions at Sea in force.

VI. Que en todos los demas aspectos el buque se ajusta a las prescripciones de las Reglas en la medida en que le son aplicables.
That in all other respects the ship complied with the requirements of the Regulations so far as these requirements apply thereto.

El presente certificado se expide con autoridad conferida por el Gobierno de la Republica de Honduras.
This certificate is issued under the authority of the Government of the Republic of Honduras.

Sera valido hasta AUGUST 16, 1998
It will remain in force until

Expedido en MANILA el 16 de MARCH de 19 98
Issued at PHILIPPINES *the* *day of*

El infrascrito declara, autorizado por el expresado Gobierno para exped
The undersigned authorised by the said Government to iss

INSPECTOR DE SURVEYOR TO HINSIB

CAPT. RUAL PINEDA

NOTA- Bastara con indicar el ano en que la quilla fue colocada o en que la construccion del buque se hallaba en una fase equivalente, salvo por lo que respecta a 1952, 1965 y 1980, casos en los que se debera consignar la fecha comleta.
NOTE- It will be sufficient to indicate the year in which the keel was laid or when the ship was at a similar stage of construction except for 1952, 1965 and 1980, in which cases the actual date should be given.

165

T.G.E. ENTERPRISE

S2-24, WISMA ABAD, JALAN HARIMAU
80250 JOHOR BAHRU, JOHOR, MALAYSIA
TEL : (607) 2227111

INVOICE
=======

FIRST ENTERPRISE CO. LTD.,
9F, NO.391 SHIN YI ROAD SEC.4
TAIPEI, TAIWAN
R.O.C.

INVOICE NO.	:	TGE/09338/98
DATE	:	16TH APRIL 1998
VESSEL NAME	:	M.T. SURIN
BILL OF LADING NO.	:	PSC/6637/98
LOADING PORT	:	INDONESIA PORT
TRANSPORTATION TO	:	KAOHSIUNG PORT, TAIWAN

DESCRIPTION OF GOODS	QUANTITY	UNIT PRICE	TOTAL

DESCRIPTION OF GOODS	QUANTITY	UNIT PRICE	TOTAL
R.B.D. PALM OLEIN IN BULK	5230.00 M/T	USD400.00 PER M/TON	USD2,092,000.00

TOTAL : TWO MILLION AND NINETY TWO THOUSAND ONLY.

FOR AND ON BEHALF OF :
T.G.E. ENTERPRISE

PETRO-PIRATES

REPUBLIK INDONESIA
REPUBLIC OF INDONESIA

NO.

SURAT IZIN BERLAYAR
PORT CLEARANCE

Untuk kapal motor/uap bernama .... Ukuran .... GT .... NT
For the motor/steam ship   burthen

berlayar dibawah bendera .... degan nakhoda ....
Sailing under   flag commanded by

bertujuan ke ....
Bound for

Dengan ini kapal tersebut diatas diizinkan berlayar
The above montioned vessel is hereby granted sailing permid

Diberikan di   :
Issued at

                            ADMINISTRATOR PELABUHAN MAKASSAR
                            KEPALA BIDANG KESYAHBANDARAN

Pada tanggal   : .... 19..........
Date   S e l a k u

Jam   : ....
Time   / HARBOUR MASTER

KANTOR ADPEL MAKASSAR   KABAG NIP 361 14744

Perhatian : Jika terdapat perobahan-perobahan dan/atau coretan, coretan maka surat izin berlayar ini tidak berlaku
Note   : Correction and / or deletion will render this document unvalid.

PPK NO. 6   SY . 82

BERLAKU S/D	JAM	
VALID UNTIL	HOURS	

PETRO-PIRATES

Certificado de Seguridad de Construcción para Buque de Carga
Cargo Ship Safety Construction Certificate

REPUBLICA DE HONDURAS
REPUBLIC OF HONDURAS

EXPEDIDO EN VIRTUD DE LAS DISPOSICIONES DEL CONVENIO INTERNACIONAL
PARA LA SEGURIDAD DE LA VIDA HUMANA EN EL MAR, 1960
*ISSUED UNDER THE PROVISIONS OF THE INTERNATIONAL CONVENTION
FOR THE SAFETY OF LIFE AT SEA. 1960*

SC 1500-

INTERIM Validity not to exceed five months
Pending issurance of full term certificate

Nombre del buque *Name of ship*	Numero o letras distintivos *Distinctive Number or letters*	Puerto de matricula *Port of Registry*	Arqueo bruto *Gross Tonnage*	Fecha en que se colocó la quilla (véase NOTA) *Date on which keel was laid (see note below)*
M.T. SURIN	HQXT 10	SAN LORENZO	3151.61MT	1985

El abajo firmante,
I, the undersigned

CAPT. RUAL PINEDA

certifica
certify

Que el buque arriba mencionado ha sido objeto de reconocimiento, de conformidad con lo dispuesto en la Regla 10 del Capitulo 1 del citado Convenio, y que dicho reconocimiento ha revelado que el estado del casco, de las máquinas y del equipo, según lo definido en la expresada Regla, es satisfactorio en todos los sentidos, y que el buque cumple con las prescripciones aplicables de las Capitulos II (sin que entren aquí las relativas a dispositivos de extincion de incendios y a planos de los sistemas de lucha contra incendios).

That the above-mentioned ship has been duly surveyed in accordance with the provisions of Regulation 10 of Chapter 1 of the Convention referred to above, and that survey showed that the condition of the hull, machinery and equipment as defined in the above Regulation, was in all respects satisfactory and that the ship complied with the applicable requirements of Chapter II (other than those relating to fire extinguishing, appliances and fire control plans).

El presente certificado se expide con autoridad conferida por el Gobierno de la Republica de Honduras.
This certificate is issued under the authority of the Government of the Republic of Honduras.

Será válido hasta. . . . . . **AUGUST 16, 1998**
It will remain in force until

Expedido en . . . **MANILA** . . . . a . . . **16** . . . de . . . **MARCH** . . . . . . de 19 **98**
Issued at . . . **PHILIPPINES** . . . . *the* . . . . *day of*

El infrascrito declara que esta . . . . torizado por el expresado
Gobierno para expedir el p . . . . ca . . . .

*The undersigned decla . . . . authorised by the said
Government to issue t . . . .*

INSPECTOR DE . . . . . OR TO HINSIB

CAPT. RUAL PINEDA

NOTA- Bastará con indicar el ano en que la quilla fue colocada o en que la construccion del buque se hallaba en una fase equivalente, salvo por lo que respecta a 1952, 1965 y 1980, casos en los que se deberá consignar la fecha completa.

NOTE- It will be sufficient to indicate the year in which the keel was laid or when the ship was at a similar stage of construction except for 1952, 1965 and 1980, in which cases the actual date should be given.

168

Appendix C

PAUL SHIPPING COMPANY
5, JALAN PERMAS 4/4
91750 PERMAS JAYA
JOHOR, MALAYSIA
TEL : 607-3351570
FAX : 607-3351570

VESSEL NAME : M.T. SURIN
VOGY. : 98
CAPT. :

NO OF SHEET : 1
FROM : INDONESIA PORT
TO : KAOHSIUNG PORT, TAIWAN
DATE : 15/4/1998

B/L NO.	SHIPPERS	CONSIGNEES	MARKS & NOS	NO OF PACKAGE	DESCRIPTION OG GOODS	WEIGHT	MEASUREMENT	FREIGHT	REMARKS
PSC/6637/98	T.G.E. ENTERPRISE S2-24, WISMA ABAD JALAN HARIMAU 80250 JOHOR BAHRU JOHOR, MALAYSIA	FIRST ENTERPRISE CO; LTD, 9F.NO.391 SHIN YI ROAD SEC. 4 TAIPEI, TAIWAN R.O.C.			R.B.D. PALM OLEIN IN BULK BY TANKER	5230.00 M/TONS			

PAUL SHIPPING COMPANY

FUERZA NAVAL DE HONDURAS
Naval Force of Honduras
SUPERINTENDENCIA DE MARINA MERCANTE NACIONAL
Superintendency of the National Merchant Marine
REGISTRO DE MATRICULA PROVISIONAL
Provisional Registry
NUM: L.-.6.6.3.4.5.8.4

El Infrascrito, Comandate General de la FUERZA NAVAL DE HONDURAS, por medio del presente documento HACE CONSTAR: que los Armadores de la Nave que se describe a continuación, han presentado la solicitud para que la misma sea matriculada en forma provisional en el Registro Maritimo respectivo, quedando en consecuencia obligados a presentar la documentación que establece la Ley, a efecto de que se le extienda a dicha Nave la correspondiente Patente Definitiva de Navegación.

The Undersigned, Commander In Chief of the Honduras Naval Force, by means of this document, HEREBY CERTIFY, that the Owners of the under-described vessel have submitted an application and applied to have the vessel provisionally registered in the Maritime Registry, undertaking to submit the documents established by the Law for obtention of the final Ship's Register Certificate to be issued to this vessel.

GENERALIDADES DE LA NAVE
General Ship's Data

NOMBRE DE LA NAVE:....M.T. SURIN...........   ARMADORES:.....SEA KING SHIPPING CO.S.DE R.L.
Ship's Name   Owners
TIPO DE LA NAVE.........OIL TANKER...........   DOMICILIO....AVE LUISE 130 BOX 60
Type of Vessel   Adress   BRUSELAS BELGICA
NACIONALIDAD ACTUAL:.....HONDURENA.......   REPRESENTANTE:..ABG..OSWALDO..DA..COSTA......
Present Nationality   Representative
LUGAR Y FECHA DE CONSTRUCCION:....JAPAN   CONTRUIDO POR:..FUKAE..ZOSEN..HOROSIMA..JAPAN
   1985

Place and Year of Built   Builder's Name:

CARACTERISTICAS PRINCIPALES
Main Particulars

	MATERIAL DEL CASCO	DIMENSIONES:	TONELAJE:
	Hull Material: X	Dimensions:	Tonnage:
NUMERO DE............	ACERO................	ESLORA....9.7..25MTS...	BRUTO......315.1..6.1MT
Number of:	Steel	Length	Gross
CUBIERTAS......DOS.	MADERA................	MANGA....16.50MTS	NETO........1365..21MT
Decks	Wood	Breadth	Net
MASTILES.....UNO	FIBRA DE VIDRIO...............	PUNTAL....7.62MTS	
Masts	Fibreglass	Depth	
CHIMENEAS....UNA	ALUMINIO..................	CALADO.....5.25MTS	
Funnels	Aluminium	Draft	
	OTROS.................		
	Others		

SISTEMA DE PROPULSION
Propulsion System
NUM. Y CLASE DE MOTORES....UNO..DIESEL....
Number and Type of Engine   6 CIL   5500 BHP
VELOCIDAD DE LA NAVE....11.2..NUDOS..............
Ship's Speed

SISTEMA DE ESTACION DE RADIO
Radio Station System
CLASE DE RADIO................
Type of Radio
INDICATIVO DE LLAMADA................
Call Sign Letters
FRECUENCIAS................
Frecuencies

EMPRESA RESPONSABLE DE OPERACION....SEA KING SHIPPING CO.S. DE R.L.
Enterprise responsible for operation
PERMISO PROVISIONAL DE NAVEGACION
NUM:....L-6634584
Provisional Navigation Permit No:
REGISTRO DE MATRICULA PROVISIONAL
NUM: ..
Provisional Ship's Register Certificate No:
EXTENDIDA EN TEGUCIGALPA, D. C. :.
Issued at Tegucigalpa, D. C. on

DATED EMITTED..16 MARCH..1998
FECHA EMISION....16 MARSO..1998
DATE OF EXPIRATION....16 AUGUST 1998
FECHA DE EXPIRACION....16 AGUSTO 1998

FECHA DE VENCIMIENTO:................
Expiring Date

COMANDANTE GENERAL FUERZA NAVAL
COMMANDER IN CHIEF NAVAL FORCE

REPUBLICA DE HONDURAS

INTERIM Validity not to exceed five months Pending issurance of full term certificate

INTERNATIONAL OIL POLLUTION PREVENTION CERTIFICATE

(This certificate shall be supplemented by a record of construction and equipment)

Issued under the provisions of the International convention for the Prevention of Pollution from ships, 1973, as modified by the Protocol of 1978 relating - thereto (hereinafter referred to as "the convention") under the authority of the Government of Honduras Republic,

by HONDURAS INTERNATIONAL NAVAL SURVEYING AND INSPECTION BUREAU
(full designation of the competent person of Organization authorized under the provisions of the convention)

name of ship	distinctive number or letters	port of registry	gross tonnage
M.T. SURIN	HQXT 10	SAN LORENZO	3151.61MT

Type of ship:

ship other than any of the above*

THIS IS TO CERTIFY:

1. That the ship has been surveyed in accordance with regulation 4 of annex I of the convention; and
2. That the survey shows that the structure, equipment, systems, fittings, arrangement and materials of the ship and the condition thereof are in all respects satisfactory and that the ship complies with the applicable requirements of annex I of the convention.

This certificate is issued under the authority of the above Government.

It will remain in force until.....AUGUST..16, 1998

Subject to surveys in accordance with regulation 4 of annex I of the convention.

Issued at   MANILA   the   16   day of   MARCH   19 98
         PHILIPPINES

....
Inspector de/surveyor to
HONDURAS INTERNATIONAL NAVAL SURVEYING
AND INSPECTION BUREAU
CAPT. RUAL PINEDA

* Delete as appropriate

Form No. 1215225-8

172

PETRO-PIRATES

CERTIFICADO INTERNACIONAL DE FRANCOBORDO (1966)

INTERNATIONAL LOAD LINE CERTIFICATE (1966)

REPUBLICA DE HONDURAS

Expedido en virtud de las disposiciones de la Convenion Internacional de 1966 sobre Lineas de Carga, en nombre del Gobierno de la Republic de Honduras por HONDURAS INTERNACIONAL DE INSPECCION Y AGRIMENSURA NAVAL

Issued under the provisions of the International Convention on Load Lines, 1966, under the authority of the Government of Honduras by the HONDURAS INTERNATIONAL NAVAL SURVEYING AND INSPECTION BUREAU

Nombre de Buque Name of Ship	Numero o letras distintivos Dinstintive Number or Letters	Puerto de Matricula Port of Registry	Eslora (L) definida art 2(8) Length (L) defined art 2(8)	Fecha en que se coloco la quilla Date on which* keel was laid
M.T. SURIN	HQXT 10	SANLORENZO	97.25MTS	1985

Francobordo asignado como: * Buque nuevo, *Buque existente
Freeboard assigned as: *A new ship; * An existing ship
Tipo de buque: * Tipo A * Tipo B con francobordo reducido/* Tipo B con francobordo aumentado
Type of ship: * Type A *Type B with * reduced/* increased freeboard

        * Tacha lo que no corresponda
        * Delete whichever is inapplicable

Francobordo medido desde la linea de cubierta
Freeboard from Deck line

			Situacion de la linea de carga / Load Line
Tropical	1026	mm (T)	142 mm por encima de (V) / above (S)
Tropical		(T)	
Verano	1266	mm (V)	Borde superior de la linea situado a la alfura del centro c anillo
Summer		(S)	Upper edge of line at the level of centre of ring
Invierno	1224	mm (I)	138 mm por debajo de (V) / below (S)
Winter	–	(W)	– mm por debajo de (V) / below (S)
Atlantico Norte Invierno	–	mm (ANI)	– mm por debajo de (V) / below (S)
Winter North Atlantic		(WNA)	
Madera, Tropical	–	mm (MT)	– mm por encima de (MV) / above (LS)
Timber, Tropical	–	(LT)	
Madera; Verano	–	mm (MV)	– mm por encima de (V) / above (S)
Timber, Summer		(LS)	
Madera, Invierno	–	mm (MI)	– mm por debajo de (MV) / below (LS)
Timber, Winter	–	(LW)	
Madera, Atlantico Norte Invierno	–	mm (MANI)	– mm por debajo de (MV) / below (LS)
Timber Winter North Atlantic		(LWNA)	

NOTA: Los francobordos y lineas de carga que no sean aplicables no necesitan ser mencionados en el certificado
Note: Freeboards and load lines which are not applicable need not be entered on the certificate.
Reduccion en agua dulce para todos los francobordos, diferentes del madera......145.....mm
Allowance for fresh water for all freeboards other than timber
Para el francobordo para madera...A?.0.mm
Fore timber freeboards
El borde superior de la marca de la linea de cubierta, desde el
cual se miden estos francobordos esta a .... de la cubierta en el costado
The upper edge of the deck line from which these freeboards are measured is   0mm above the top   deck at side
Fecha de la visita inicial o periodica ..MARCH..16.........19.98.......   steel upper
Date of initial or periodical survey

R O H E (load line mark)

Se certifica que esta buque ha sido visitado y que han sido asignados los francobordos y se han marcado las lineas de carga anteriormente indicadas de acuerdo con lo dispuesto en el Convenio Internacional sobre Lines de Carga de 1966.
This is to certify that this ship has been surveyed and that the freeboards have been assigned and load lines shown above have been marked in accordance with the international Convention on Load Lines 1966.

Esta certificado es valido hasta
This certificate is valid until

sometido a Inspecciones periodicas de conformidad, con el Articulo 14(1) (c) del Convenio
Subject to periodical Inspection in accordance with Article 14(1) (c) of the Convention.

Expedido en MANILA.............el ..16. de AUGUST. 19..98...
Issued at, PHILIPPINES

El infrascrito declara que esta debidamente autorizado por el expresado Gobierno para expedir el presente certificato.
The undersigned declares that he is duly authorised by the said Government to issue this certificate.

....
Inspector del Surveyor to
HONDURAS INTERNATIONAL NAVAL SURVEYING
AND INSPECTION BUREAU

CAPT. RUAL PINEDA

Sera suficiente que se indique el ano en que la quilla fue colocada o en que la construccion de buque se hallaba en una fase equivalente, salvo por lo que respecta a 1968 caso en el que se debera consignar la fecha completa.
It will be sufficient to indicate the year in which the keel was laid or when the ship was at a similar stage of construction except for 1968, in which case the actual date should be given.

Form No: 1215225-1

173

PETRO-PIRATES

CODE NAME: "CONGENBILL" . EDITION 1978

Shipper

T.G.E. ENTERPRISE
32 JALAN NAGASARI 16
SEGAMAT BARU, 85000
SEGAMAT, JOHOR, MALAYSIA

B/L No:

PSC/6637/98

Consignee

FIRST ENTERPRISE CO. LTD.,
9F, NO.391 SHIN YI ROAD SEC.4
TAIPEI, TAIWAN
R.O.C.

Notify address

SAME AS CONSIGNEE

PAUL SHIPPING COMPANY
Bill of Lading

RECEIVED in apparent good order and condition except as otherwise noted that total number of Containers of Packages or units enumerated below for transportation from the place of receipt to the place of delivery subject to the terms hereof. One of the original Bills of Lading must be surrendered duly endorsed in exchange for the Goods or Delivery Order. On presentation of this document (duly endorsed) to the Carrier by or on behalf of the Holder, the rights and liabilities in accordance with the terms hereof shall (without prejudice to any rule of common law or statute rendering them binding on the (Merchant) become binding in all respects between the Carrier and the Holder as though the contract evidenced hereby had been made between them.
IN WITNESS whereof the number of original Bills of Lading stated below have been signed, one of which being accomplished, the other(s) to be void.

SEE TERMS ON REVERSE

Vessel **Port of loading**

M.T. SURIN   INDONESIA PORT

Port of discharge

KAOHSIUNG PORT, TAIWAN

Shipper's description of goods

NON-NEGOTIABLE COPY

Gross weight

R.B.D. PALM OLEIN
IN BULK BY TANKER

NET WEIGHT

5230.00 M/TONS

FREIGHT PREPAID

SHIPPED ON BOARD   15 APR 1998

TOTAL : FIVE THOUSAND TWO HUNDRED AND THIRTY M/TONS ONLY.

Freight payable as per
CHARTER-PARTY dated

FREIGHT ADVANCE.
Received on account of freight:

Time used for loading _____ days _____ hours.

SHIPPED at the Port of Loading in apparent good order and condition on board the Vessel for carriage to the Port of Discharge or so near thereto as she may safely get the goods specified above.
Weight, measure, quality, quantity, condition, contents and value unknown.
IN WITNESS whereof the Master or Agent of the said Vessel has signed the number of Bills of Lading indicated below all of this tenor and date, any one of which being accomplished the others shall be void.

FOR CONDITIONS OF CARRIAGE SEE OVERLEAF

Freight payable at	Place and date of issue
MALAYSIA	MALAYSIA 15/4/1998
Number of original Bs/L	Signature
THREE (3) ONLY.	PAUL SHIPPING COMPANY
	As Agent

PETRO-PIRATES

BILL OF LADING

TO BE USED WITH CHARTER-PARTIES
CODE NAME: "CONGENBILL"
EDITION 1978
ADOPTED BY
THE BALTIC AND INTERNATIONAL
MARITIME CONFERENCE (BIMCO)

Conditions of Carriage.

(1) All terms and conditions, liberties and exceptions of the Charter Party, dated as overleaf, are herewith incorporated. The Carrier shall in no case be responsible for loss of or damage to cargo arisen prior to loading and after discharging.

(2) **General Paramount Clause.**
The Hague Rules contained in the International Convention for the Unification of certain rules relating to Bills of Lading, dated Brussels the 25th August 1924 as enacted in the country of shipment shall apply to this contract. When no such enactment is in force in the country of shipment, the corresponding legislation of the country of destination shall apply, but in respect of shipments to which no such enactments are compulsorily applicable, the terms of the said Convention shall apply.

Trades where Hague-Visby Rules apply.
In trades where the International Brussels Convention 1924 as amended by the Protocol signed at Brussels on February 23rd 1968 – the Hague-Visby Rules – apply compulsorily, the provisions of the respective legislation shall be considered incorporated in this Bill of Lading. The Carrier takes all reservations possible under such applicable legislation, relating to the period before loading and after discharging and while the goods are in the charge of another Carrier, and to deck cargo and live animals.

(3) **General Average.**
General Average shall be adjusted, stated and settled according to York-Antwerp Rules 1974, in London unless another place is agreed in the Charter.

Cargo's contribution to General Average shall be paid to the Carrier even when such average is the result of a fault, neglect or error of the Master, Pilot or Crew. The Charterers, Shippers and Consignees expressly renounce the Netherlands Commercial Code, Art. 700, and the Belgian Commercial Code, Part II, Art. 148.

(4) **New Jason Clause.**
In the event of accident, danger, damage or disaster before or after the commencement of the voyage, resulting from any cause whatsoever, whether due to negligence or not, for which, or for the consequence of which, the Carrier is not responsible, by statute, contract or otherwise, the goods, Shippers, Consignees or owners of the goods shall contribute with the Carrier in general average to the payment of any sacrifices, losses or expenses of a general average nature that may be made or incurred and shall pay salvage and special charges incurred in respect of the goods.

If a salving ship is owned or operated by the Carrier, salvage shall be paid for as fully as if the said salving ship or ships belonged to strangers. Such deposit as the Carrier or his agents may deem sufficient to cover the estimated contribution of the goods and any salvage and special charges thereon shall, if required, be made by the goods, Shippers, Consignees or owners of the goods to the Carrier before delivery.

(5) **Both-to-Blame Collision Clause.**
If the Vessel comes into collision with another ship as a result of the negligence of the other ship and any act, neglect or default of the Master, Mariner, Pilot or the servants of the Carrier in the navigation or in the management of the Vessel, the owners of the cargo carried hereunder will indemnify the Carrier against all loss or liability to the other or non-carrying ship or her Owners in so far as such loss or liability represents loss of, or damage to, or any claim whatsoever of the owners of said cargo, paid or payable by the other or non-carrying ship or her Owners to the owners of said cargo and set-off, recouped or recovered by the other or non-carrying ship or her Owners as part of their claim against the carrying Vessel or Carrier. The foregoing provisions shall also apply where the Owners, operators or those in charge of any ship or ships or objects other than, or in addition to, the colliding ships or objects are at fault in respect of a collision or contact.

For particulars of cargo, freight,
destination, etc., see overleaf.

PETRO-PIRATES

ENDORSEMENT FOR ANNUAL AND INTERMEDIATE SURVEYS

THIS IS TO CERTIFY that a survey required by regulation 4 of annex I of the convention the ship was found to comply with the relevant provisions of the convention:

Annual survey: signed...
                                   (signature of duly authorized
                                                official)

                                   place..

                                   date...
              (seal or stamp of the Authority, as appropriate)

Annual*/intermediate*/survey: signed...
          unschedules*   (signature of duly authorized
                                                official)

                                   place..

                                   date...
              (seal or stamp of the Authority, as appropriate)

Annual*/intermediate*/survey: signed...
          unschedules*   (signature of duly authorized
                                                official)

                                   place..

                                   date...
              (seal or stamp of the Authority, as appropriate)

Annual-survey: signed...
          unschedules *   (Signature of duly authorized
                                                official)

                                   place..

                                   date...
              (seal or stamp of the Authority, as appropriate)

* Delete as appropriate

176

PETRO-PIRATES

NOTAS

1. Cuando un buque parta de un puerto situado en un rio o en aguas interiores se le permitira cargar hasta un calado mayor correspondiente al peso de combustible y otras provisiones necessarias para el consumo entre el punto de salida y la mar.

2. Cuando un buque navergue en agua dulce de densidad igual a la unidad la linea de carga correspondiente podra sumerguse en al cantidad correspondiente a la concesion para agua dulce indicada anteriormente. Cuando la densidad sea diferente de la unidad se hara una conceston proporcional a la diferencia entire 1.025 y la densidad real.

NOTES:

1. When a ship departs from a port situated on a river or inland waters, deeper loading shall be permitted corresponding to the weight of fuel and all other materials required for consumption between the point of departure and the sea.

2. When a ship is in fresh water of unit density the appropriate load line may be submerged by the amount of the fresh water allowance shown above. Where the density is other than unity, an allowance shall be made proportional to the difference between 1.025 and the actual density.

Se certifica que en la inspeccio'n prevista en el Articulo 14 (1) (c) del Convenio, este buque cumpila las precripciones del convenio
This is to certify that at a periodical inspection required by Article 14 (1) (c) of the Convention this ship was found to comply with the relevant provisions of the Convention.

En MANILA PHILIPPINES Fecha .... 16 FEBRUARY 1998 ....
Place .... Date

Firma del Inspector de
_____ Honduras International Naval Surveying and Inspection Bureau
Signature of the Surveyor to

En .... Fecha ....
Place .... Date

Firma del Inspector de
_____ Honduras International Naval Surveying and Inspection Bureau
Signature of the Surveyor to

En .... Fecha ....
Place .... Date

Firma del Inspector de
_____ Honduras International Naval Surveying and Inspection Bureau
Signature of the Surveyor to

En .... Fecha ....
Place .... Date

Firma del Inspector de
_____ Honduras International Naval Surveying and Inspection Bureau
Signature of the Surveyor to

Habiento cumplido este buque por completo las prescripciones del Convenio, se prorroga la validez de este certificado, de acuerdo con el Articulo 19 (2) del Convenio, hasta ....

The provisions of the Convention being fully complied with by this ship, the validity of this certificate is, in accordance with Article 19 (2) of the Convention, extended until ....

En .... Fecha ....
Place .... Date

....
HONDURAS INTERNATIONAL NAVAL SURVEYING
AND INSPECTION BUREAU

177

Appendix D

Factsheet

ICC COMMERCIAL CRIME SERVICES

International Maritime Bureau (IMB)

Background

Fraud, cargo theft, piracy, the deviation of ships from legitimate destinations, the illegal dumping of toxic waste at sea, and potential cruise liner terrorism are all facets of a new growth industry - crime in international trade. No one knows how much it costs industry but it is certainly millions of dollars every day.

The consequences can be devastating to insurers, banks, traders, shipowners and charterers. They are of direct concern to bankers, lawyers and maritime surveyors, to name but a few.

Purpose

To counter crime in international trade, the International Chamber of Commerce (ICC) established the International Maritime Bureau (IMB) in 1981. The Bureau now forms part of ICC Commercial Crime Services.

Support for the IMB came soon after its creation in the form of a resolution at the regular session of the United Nations' International Maritime Organisation urging "all interests and organisations concerned to co-operate fully with the International Chamber of Commerce and its International Maritime Bureau in taking effective measures for the prevention of maritime fraud".

The IMB is a non-profit organisation, with members in 75 countries. It enjoys the formal support and co-operation of the governments and law enforcement agencies of the world's trading nations.

The Bureau's central objective is to contain and prevent fraud and malpractice, particularly in the commercial sector.

INTERNATIONAL CHAMBER OF COMMERCE
The world business organisation
38, Cours Albert 1er - 75008 Paris, France
Tel. (33)(1) 49.53.28.28; Telex 650770 F
Fax (33)(1) 49.53.29.42 / 49.53.28.59

For more information on the International Maritime Bureau, please contact:
Eric Ellen, Executive Director
ICC Commercial Crime Services
Tel (44)(0181) 591.30.00
Fax (44)(0181) 594.2833

Services

In an age where companies are being forced to apply an ever increasing degree of due diligence to their operating practices, IMB services - advisory, preventive and responsive - can be invaluable. They are available through the Bureau's, multilingual, multi-disciplinary staff. The Bureau will respond to identified needs either on its own initiative or on behalf of specific parties.

Information is the key to fraud prevention. The Bureau maintains confidential databases on all aspects of trading fraud. A twice-monthly bulletin on recent defaulters, companies in financial trouble and malpractices in trading and shipping is sent to members and provides an essential aid to minimising risks. This is backed by a credit reporting service where some 12,000 reports on companies engaged in shipping related activities are available through an on-line service.

Prevention services include the authentification of trading documents. They are widely used by banks and traders. The Bureau examines suspect documents, including bills of lading involving million dollar sums. Many are shown to be false.

The Bureau also operates a cargo loss reporting centre which identifies loss patterns involving specific companies, individuals and commodities in order to target specific risk areas.

The ship monitoring and supercargo service have been supplemented by the creation of the Chartering Experience Programme under which the credentials of prospective charterers are checked before a vessel is fixed.

Probably the greater part of the Bureau's work is responsive. The Bureau's investigations cover all aspects of crime and malpractice from the disappearance of ships and cargoes to diverse aspects of maritime fraud in all its forms. The investigations uncover not only individual crimes but also repetitive organised crime on an international scale.

The Bureau will also act as an independent intermediary in commercial disputes where it will negotiate on behalf of interested parties in cases where litigation may not be a cost-effective alternative.

The services of Bureau staff are being used increasingly for expert witness functions on all aspects of maritime casualties and particularly in cases of cargo loss.

Far East Regional Office

The Far East regional office in Kuala Lumpur covers the full range of IMB activities and is run on the same lines as the head office in London. A regional piracy centre was added in October, 1992 as an industry response to the increase in piracy in Far Eastern waters. The piracy centre has significantly contributed to the reduction in piratical attacks in the Malacca Straits.

The ICC and the IMB

The ICC, the world business organisation, complements the practical work of the IMB through its commissions on international commercial practice and maritime and surface transport.

The ICC, with members in 140 countries enjoys first category consultative status with the United Nations and other inter-governmental bodies.

Lectures and training

Much of the Bureau's preventive work is in the form of lectures and training. The Bureau organises seminars, workshops and lectures focusing on topics of interest to the international maritime and trading communities. It will also undertake in-house training assignments on request.

Publications

IMB Confidential Bulletin is published twice monthly and is available free and exclusively to members.

ICC Commercial Crime International is a monthly review, free to members but available on subscription to the general public.

IMB Special Report is an in-depth examination of problem areas in trading and shipping. Recent reports have included "Due Diligence", "Container Crime", "Nigeria - Traders at risk". These publications are available from ICC Publishing SA, 38, Cours Albert 1er, 75008 Paris, from ICC national committees, as well as from ICC Commercial Crime Services.

Organisation

The IMB is one of three units comprising ICC Commercial Crime Services, a specialised division dealing with all aspects of crime affecting business. ICC Commercial Crime Services is headed by Eric Ellen, Executive Director, former Chief Constable, Port of London Police.

ICC COMMERCIAL CRIME SERVICES

International Maritime Bureau
Maritime House
1 Linton Road - Barking, Essex
1G11 8HG United Kingdom
Tel. (44-0181) 591.30.00
Telex: 8956492 IMBLDN G
Fax: (44-0181) 594.2833

PETRO-PIRATES

ICC - INTERNATIONAL MARITIME BUREAU

MARITIME HOUSE, 1 LINTON RD, BARKING, ESSEX, IG11 8HG, U.K.
TEL: +44 181 591 3000 FAX: +44 181 594 2833 TLX: 8956492 IMBLDN G
E MAIL ccst@dial.pinex.com

TOTAL NUMBER OF PAGES: 3

DATE	: 08 April 1999
TO	: Capt Ken Blyth
FAX	: 00 61 7 55 73 1349

PIRACY - PETRO RANGER

Dear Capt Blyth,

I refer to your fax of 23 March 99 addressed to Capt Mukundan and apologise for the delay in responding.

Our 1998 piracy report has been mailed to you today. It is rather bulky to fax. If you need any particular aspect in a hurry please advise and I shall fax you the information.

We have taken up the issue of hijackings at the Maritime Safety Committee of IMO. I have attached a copy of our submission which will be discussed by the Committee which meets next month (19 to 28 May 1999). You may wish to ask your government to endorse our views at the Meeting.

Regards and please do keep in touch.

Yours sincerely

Capt Jayant Abhyankar
Deputy Director

PETRO-PIRATES

MARITIME SAFETY COMMITTEE, 71st SESSION, AGENDA ITEM 15

PIRACY AND ARMED ROBBERY AGAINST SHIPS

REPORT OF SERIOUS INCIDENTS

Submitted by the International Maritime Bureau (IMB) of the International Chamber of Commerce (ICC).

SUMMARY
Executive Summary: This document contains reports of three violent incidents of piracy in 1998. There is a growing trend in violence and in some cases murdering of the innocent seamen. The document also highlights the urgent need for the law enforcement to treat piracy as a serious offence and prosecute the pirates.
Action to be taken : Paragraph 5.
Related documents : MSC71/15

1. During 1998, the Piracy Reporting Centre of the ICC International Maritime Bureau has received 15 reports of vessels being hijacked by pirates. These attacks are getting more violent including murder of the innocent crew members.

2. The case of the PETRO RANGER is representative of these hijackings. What makes this case important is that although the alleged pirates, the ship and her cargo were found intact, the pirates were not prosecuted and repatriated to their home country.

2.1 M V PETRO RANGER sailed from Singapore on 16 April 1998 with a cargo of gas oil and Kerosene. Nine hours later, she was boarded by 12 armed pirates. The crew were forced to sail the vessel to Hainan island in China. The 22 crew members under control of the pirates were threatened with death and remained locked in the mess room for ten days.

2.2 The local authorities alleged that the vessel was engaged in smuggling operations. They detained and questioned the crew for over two weeks, seized the vessel and confiscated the cargo. They questioned the 12 alleged pirates who were carrying Indonesian travel documents. However, on 15 October 1998, despite indisputable evidence, the 12 pirates who had committed a serious offence of hijacking of the vessel and an attempt to illegally sell the cargo, were sent back to Indonesia without being prosecuted.

2.3 It is submitted that piracy cannot be resolved in this way. This incident will encourage the pirates to carry on, knowing that in some jurisdictions they can extricate themselves out of difficult situations.

3. The second incident involved M.V TENYU, a Panama flagged general cargo vessel. She loaded a cargo of 3,006 MT Aluminium ingots in bundles at Kuala Tanjong for South Korea on 27 September 1998. Thereafter she went missing with her 15 crew members from South Korea and China. On 21 December 1998, the TENYU was subsequently found in the port of Zhang Jia Gang, China. She was operating under the name of SANEI 1 with a crew consisting of 14 Indonesians. The original crew consisting of two South Koreans and 13 Chinese are feared murdered by the pirates.

3.1 The IMB discovered that one of the 14 Indonesian crew on board the SANEI 1 was also an alleged pirate on board the ANNA SIERRA which was hijacked in September 1995. At that time this crew member and others were sent home by the Chinese authorities despite irrefutable evidence of their complicity in the hijacking of the ANNA SIERRA. The case of ANNA SIERRA was earlier reported by the IMB to the Maritime Safety Committee, 66th Session in June 1996. It is hoped that on this occasion, the 14 Indonesians found on board the SANEI 1 will be prosecuted and not again sent home without charge by the Chinese authorities.

3.2 On a positive note the IMB wishes to make a special mention of the following organisations for their excellent work in locating the TENYU.

- Zhang Jia Gang Harbour Superintendency Administration (HSA)
- China Maritime Search and Rescue Center
- Maritime Safety Administration (MSA) of the People's Republic of China.

4. The third incident involves M.V CHEUNG SON, a Panama flagged Bulk Carrier. She loaded a cargo of furnace slag in China for Malaysia. She went missing on 16 November 1998, about 200 miles east of Hong Kong in South China Sea. Her 23 Chinese crew members were murdered by the pirates. The Chinese police have reportedly arrested 20 persons suspected of being the pirates. They have confessed to the authorities that they gathered the crew together on the deck and shot them. The bodies were said to have been weighted, bound and gagged. Six bodies were recovered in the nets of Chinese fishing boats off the Southern Chinese port of Shantou.

Action Requested by the Committee

5. Due to an unacceptable growing level of violence, there is an urgent need for the Committee to take note of the above incidents and to consider if there are any recommendations for dealing with similar situations.

PETRO-PIRATES

Petroships
Pte Ltd

460 Alexandra Road
#25-04 PSA Building
Singapore 119963

Telephone : 273 1122
Telex : RS 24176
Fax : 273 2200

23 April 1998

To   : Capt. Ahmad Bin Othman
       Director
       Safety of Navigation Division
Cc   : MRCC, Port Klang
       Capt. Prasab
Fm   : Capt. James Jerris

M.T. "PETRO RANGER" – MISSING VESSEL

We have not been able to establish contact with the vessel since Friday 17 April 98.
We have received numerous enquiries from concerned next-of-kin of the crew of the
"Petro Ranger" and we are ourselves very concerned about the whereabouts and safety
of the vessel and crew. We suspect that the vessel has been hijacked.

We have been in contact with the Royal Australian Airforce both in Australia and at
Butterworth, Penang. We are aware that the Australian Airforce based at Butterworth had
undertaken air search in the South China Sea.

From industry sources, we have learnt that in past similar cases the "hijacked" ships were
reported heading towards the Gulf of Thailand where the oil cargo was discharged.

As such, a pattern can be established where the "Petro Ranger" may also have been
"hijacked" and could possibly be in that area.

We would greatly appreciate any information and assistance you can provide us in
establishing the whereabouts of the vessel and crew. Could we also through your
good office seek assistance from the Royal Malaysian Airforce to carry out air search in
the Gulf of Thailand. I attach herewith the ship's full description plus photographs for
this purpose.

Regards

Capt. James Jeeris

184

PETRO-PIRATES

Petroships Pte Ltd

480 Alexandra Road,
#25-04 PSA Building
Singapore 119963

Telephone : 273 1122
Telex : RS 24176
Fax : 273 2200

Date: 24 April 1998

To : Ministry of Foreign Affairs
Consular Division
Attn: Mohd. Arif Kassim
Fax : 02-03-2415528

Cc : Honorary Consular
Malaysian High Commission
Singapore
Attn: Mr. Abdul Rahim bin Jaafar, 3rd Secretary Consular
Fax : 7336135

Cc : ..
Australian Defence Adviser
Australian High Commission
Singapore

Fax :   No. of Sheets : 4

<u>*TOP URGENT (PRIVATE AND CONFIDENTIAL)*</u>

Dear Sir,

RE : PETRO RANGER MISSING

We refer to our telephone conversation this morning regarding the above matter. For your information Mr. Zainal Abidin of the Embassy of Malaysia in Hanoi contacted us yesterday evening and we have faxed him the relevant information.

We have still not received any communication from the vessel. We have written to the Capt. Ahmad Bin Othman Director Safety of Navigation detailing the events of the incident. Attached are copies of the letter, crew list and ship's particulars.

We seek your assistance to locate the vessel by informing the Embassy of Malaysia in Bangkok, Phnom Penh, Manila and Jakarta. We would also appreciate it if you could also advise the Embassies to contact the local authorities in their areas to alert their Coast Guard. We have passed 8 coloured copies of the vessel to Mr. Abdul Rahim for forwarding to the respective parties.

We have also informed the Australian High Commission in Singapore and provided them the necessary details.

If you require further information kindly contact:-

Capt. Johnny Liew Tel: 02-2731122(O) Fax: 02-2732200

Thank you.
Capt. Johnny Liew
Marine Superintendent

PETRO-PIRATES

PetroshipS Pte Ltd

460 Alexandra Road
#25-04 PSA Building
Singapore 119963

Telephone : 273 1122
Telex : RS 24178
Fax : 273 2200

Date: 26 April 1998

To : Regional Piracy Centre
Kuala Lumpur
Attn: Mr. Muthu
Fax : 02-03-2385769

TOP URGENT

Dear Sir,

RE : PETRO RANGER MISSING

We refer to our telephone conversation this morning regarding the above matter. For your information we have received unconfirmed reports from vessels passing in the vicinity regarding sightings of a vessel drifting around the position 11DEG 45MIN North 119DEG 30MIN East around the Calamian Group Islands this morning 26 April 1998 at1130 hours.

We would highly appreciate if you could relay the information to the relevant authorities to make a search in the area.

Thank you.
Capt. Johnny Liew
Marine Superintendent

cc. Shipet Maritime Sdn Bhd/Capt Chin/Fax: 02-06-6479200

bcc. /Australian Defence Adviser /Fax:

bcc. Pacific Rescue Coordination Centre /Fax: 0011-808-541-212

186

PETRO-PIRATES

Lorraine, Richard

From:	Mo Anwar
Sent:	Wednesday, 22 April 1998 0:47
To:	Banks, Bill; McKay, Bob; Blower, Chris; Lindesay, Chris; Gray, David; Harrod, David; Ip, Edward; Le Clercq, Frank; Warfield, Ian; Holden, Jeff; Price, Jerry; Mallows, Jim; Briggs, John; Baisdon, Mike; Lorraine, Richard; Gehling, Rob; Timms, Roger; tjd@amsa.gov.au; trevor.rose@amsa.gov.au
Subject:	re: Ship Missing. (May be pirated) Captain of the ship is from Australia. Please help me to find my brother.

Hello,
I got reply from Lloyds Register. Below you will find all the information
about the ship.

****

Thanks and best regards

Mo Anwar   E-mail:moanwar@ti.com
Product Support
HDD Operations, Mixed Signal Products
Texas Instrument Inc.   Voice:(972)-997-3340
8360 LBJ Freeway, MS 8202
Dallas, TX 75243

Lloyds Register is unfortunately unable to assist you.
LR is a classification society and hence neither owns nor operates ships.

Ship movement information is totally dependant upon the last port call
information.

>From our records the ship is registered in Malaysia (Port Kelang),
is classed with NK the Japanese Classification Society
is operated under Malaysian Flag by Enerfrate Sdn Bhd of:
1st fl, Wisma MCA, 483 Jalan Bahru, Port Dickson, Malaysia
Tel: 06 647 9202 fax: 06 647 9200
and is owned by Petroships Pte. of
25-04, PSA building, 460 Alexandra Road, Singapore
Tel: 273 1122 Fax: 273 2200

The ships Sat Com Identifier is 653314010.

The Malaysian Marine Department in KL may be able to assist.

LR wishes you good luck in your search.

Graham Marshall
Marine Business Group

Original text

From: Mo Anwar <moanwar@ti.com>, on 4/20/98 11:58 PM:
To: david.harrod@amsa.gov.au, ian.warfield@amsa.gov.au,
roger.timms@amsa.gov.au, trevor.rose@amsa.gov.au, edward.ip@amsa.gov.au,
john.briggs@amsa.gov.au, richard.lorraine@amsa.gov.au, jim.mallows@amsa.gov.au,
jeff.holden@amsa.gov.au, jerry.price@amsa.gov.au, frank.leclercq@amsa.gov.au,
bob.mckay@amsa.gov.au, rob.gehling@amsa.gov.au, mike.baisdon@amsa.gov.au,
chris.lindesay@amsa.gov.au, bill.banks@amsa.gov.au, chris.blower@amsa.gov.au,
david.gray@amsa.gov.au, tjd@amsa.gov.au

PETRO-PIRATES

Last Updated

ID Numbers
  IMO Number   9052525
  Call Sign

SHIP'S NAME
  Current Name   PETRO RANGER
  Previous Name   0
  Original Name   PETRO RANGER

  Current Flag   SNG   Singapore, Republic of
  Previous Flag
  Original Flag   SNG   Singapore, Republic of

  Registered Owner   0
  Current Owner   PETROSHIPS PTE LTD
  Owner domicile   SNG   Singapore, Republic of
                        F3-Print   PgUp/PgD
                            F10-Exit

188

PETRO-PIRATES

```
v p4_0 (rdl)                    PRODUCTION SYSTEM              22 APR 98
SeabaseShip                         SHIPSYS
SEABASE ENTRY FOR: PETRO RANGER                                     2/5


  Previous Owner              0
  Previous Domicile


  Original Owner              PETROSHIPS PTE LTD
  Original Domicile           SNG          Singapore, Republic of

TONNAGE
  Gross tonnage               6718
  Net tonnage                 4023
  Deadweight tonnage (tonnes) 12357

CLASSIFICATION
  Classification Society      K            Nippon Kaiji Kyokai (Japan)
  Date of Classif (mmyy)
  Vessel Group                3            TANKERS
  Vessel Type                 TR           Oil Tankship

HULL
                F3-Print                                PgUp/PgD
                         F10-Exit
```

Index

INDEX